To Tala –

TRIUMPH

Taming the Monster within

With Love
Ingrid

INGRID KERN

First published by Dog Ear Publishing
4011 Vincennes Rd
Indianapolis, IN 46268
www.dogearpublishing.net

ISBN: 978-1-4575-4991-5

This book is printed on acid-free paper.

Printed in the United States of America

Dedication:

To my Father. Thank you, Papa, for coming to my rescue and saving my life once, giving me strength to conquer the darkness yet another time, and last, but not least, making me finish what I started. It made me understand that you, too, had to deal with your monsters and unfortunately were unable to tame them during your lifetime.

To my Mother. Thank you, Mutti, for being true to yourself and taking care of my sister and me through all the humiliation you endured, which I saw as weakness. How wrong I was.

Acknowledgements:

I thank my coach for showing me the way and making me into a competitive athlete again.

I extend my hand in gratitude to my spiritual teachers at Agape, who opened my mind, my heart and my soul.

A great big thank you to all my friends, who have stood behind me and beside me; supported and comforted me; held me in their arms throughout this journey; and helped me to gain self-confidence.

My gratitude to Master Inji Young, whose wisdom guided me and gave me the power to freeing myself from the past.

I am deeply honored to have such loyal friends. Thank you from the bottom of my heart.

Cover by Willow Raven
Author's photo by Hana Ardelean
Photo at the finish line by Peggy Bruen
Sprinting photos by Master Inji Young
Other photos from author's photo album

Part of the proceeds of my book will be donated to

Alternative House

Alternative House

Helping abused, homeless, pregnant, and at-risk youth write a second story

Alternative House opened its doors in 1972 as a small shelter for runaway teenagers in the town of Vienna, Virginia, across the river from Washington DC. It has expanded to offer residential centers and community-based services that come at a critical juncture in the lives of young people. Services are voluntary and free of charge for abused, homeless, pregnant, or at-risk youth and their families. Serving youth from elementary school students to homeless youth in their early twenties, Alternative House seeks to provide safe havens, offer opportunities to grow and thrive, step in at critical moments, and stay the course.

Every day of the week, Alternative House transforms the lives of young people. To learn more about Alternative House, or to make a charitable donation, please visit www.thealternativehouse.org.

Some measure success not by how far they have come, but in the adversity they overcame to get there. It takes courage to pick up the pen, begin a new storyline, and create a very different kind of ending.

The Past

Vienna, 1959. The phone rang. I was sitting in our living room eating breakfast, ready to go to school. I heard my mother go from the kitchen into the hallway and answer the phone. "Yes, of course, I can come by the school any time you want me to." *Oh boy, what did I do again?* Or better, *What didn't I do?* Mutti, as I called her, came into the living room and told me that the gym teacher wanted to see her. *What on earth could that be about? Gym? Of all the subjects in school!* I was a very good athlete, and I couldn't imagine what my teacher would have to tell my mother.

We both took the tram to school in the 8th district, and my mother walked me to the principal's office. I was not invited to stay with my mother; I was supposed to leave and attend class. My mother asked me to stay with her, so I could hear what was discussed. The principal gently denied my mother's wish, and I had to leave. I left the office and stood outside in the hallway, eagerly waiting for my mother to come back out. My gym teacher walked by, gave me a stern look, and told me to go to my class. She went into the office, and I didn't leave. Nervously I counted the minutes, looked at the clock on the wall and felt my heart beating against my chest. Finally, my mother came out. She looked at me with a big smile on her face, and I asked her what happened. She told me that the gym teacher asked her for permission to submit me as a participant in the 1960 Olympic preliminary tryout for the 100 meters, the long jump and the shot put. I wanted to scream for joy! I didn't expect that. OMG – how exciting! I felt an incredible surge of energy rush through my entire body, and my face probably lit up like a Christmas tree. I felt my mother's eyes looking at me with pride, and we both smiled. I asked her what her answer was, and she told me that, of course, it depended on Dad. Immediately my heart sank.

She left the school after giving me a kiss, and I went to class. Thoughts of even being considered made me feel I was on Cloud 9.

This happened in the middle of the week, and I had to wait for my father to come home for the weekend on Saturday afternoon. I normally dreaded the thought that he came home; this time, though, I was hanging out the window, searching for his car to turn the corner. Finally, he arrived. I turned away from the window, ran to the front door, down the stairs, out the building and stopped short behind my father, who was bending down to get his attaché case from the trunk. I felt like singing when I said, "Hello, Dad." He turned to me, and the look on his face quieted me immediately.

"What are you so happy about? Take the case and this bag and bring them upstairs." Oh, how I hated him at that moment. Why was he always so miserable? We both went upstairs into the apartment, where my mother was waiting at the open door, drying her hands with a kitchen towel.

"What is going on? Why is everybody so anxious?"

"Hello." Mother greeted Dad and held her face in his direction to get a kiss, which he ignored. He definitely was not in the greatest mood.

We stood in the foyer, and I waited for my mother to say something. I glanced at her, and her facial expression told me that it was not the right time to say anything, anything at all. So I took the case and the bag into my parent's room and made myself disappear. After I heard the front door close, I walked out and into the kitchen, where my mother was preparing dinner. She faced the wall and didn't turn around as she said, "Dad went to the restaurant to have a beer."

I knew she was crying and didn't want me to see it. I went to my room and tried to read but couldn't focus. All I was thinking about was telling my father the news. Time went by ever so slowly, and I didn't know what to do with myself. I looked at books and then out the window and then opened my drawers, rummaging through my sweaters. I got up, sat down, tried to read. I was a nervous wreck.

After a couple of hours, Mutti came into my room and asked me to get Dad. I walked to the restaurant, glanced through one of the windows and saw my Dad sitting there, drinking and laughing with a couple of men. I turned away from the window, then walked through the door toward my father and looked at him. He immediately saw me and yelled, "What are you doing here? Are you spying on me?" The men laughed.

"Mutti asked me to get you; dinner is ready."

"I am coming when I am finished, and I am not finished yet. You will have to wait for me." Again, laughter. I felt the eyes of the men on my back when I walked out, and I was furious. I felt like hitting him, which of course, I could only dream of doing.

Mutti, my little sister and I waited for quite a while, lounging around on the sofa without saying a word until my Dad finally appeared at home. I smelled the alcohol on his breath, and I felt disgust; my skin was crawling up my spine.

We all sat down at the dinner table, and Mutti served the soup. At first, we were silent. But then my Dad's voice was like thunder. "What is going on? What did Ingrid do again?"

"Nothing, she didn't do anything. Her gym teacher wants to submit her for the preliminary Olympic tryouts…"

"No!"

I dropped my soup spoon onto my plate and at the same time screamed, "No? Why not?"

I didn't have time to say another word before I felt his hand on my face, left and right and left and right again. I slipped off the chair and fell to the floor, crying, screaming. Then his body was over me, and he kicked my back while yelling, "You will do what I tell you to do! And if I say 'No,' then it is 'No,' and don't you ever question my reasons." He picked me up and threw me onto the chair. His voice shook as he said, "And now you eat your dinner or you go to bed without any."

I whimpered in pain while tears streamed down my face. And then – another attack. Smack! Right onto my neck and face. I lifted my arm to protect me, moved my body away from his hand and screamed, "I hate you! I hate you."

Within a split second his body loomed over me again. His hands pulled my shoulders as he shook me and yelled, "You worthless piece of garbage! One more word, and you will regret that for the rest of your life!"

I stared at him and didn't make a sound. He let go of my body, and I sat on my chair, shaking.

Nobody spoke another word for the rest of the dinner, after which I went to bed. The couple of times I attempted to ask my mother why, she shook her head and turned away from me. The last time I started to ask, she put one of her fingers on her mouth, looked at me and shook her head, which meant, don't ask. That was it. That was it!

My dream to run in another competition, even trying out, was crushed, shattered, buried. At first I would sneak to the track. Unfortunately my father was spying on me, and one day he stood behind the fence and gave me a look like he wanted the earth to open up and swallow me.

Of course, he didn't have to say one word; I knew what I had to do. I didn't even finish my long jump. I went over to my teacher to let her know that my Dad was here to pick me up, and she nodded. Turning my back, I bent down, picked up my little jacket, cursed my father under my breath, stood up and walked over to him. I was lucky that other people were around, so he didn't beat me. That was the last time I was at a track for – what seemed to be – another lifetime.

2004, Los Angeles. I was at a gathering with a group of people from the Austrian American Council West and having a conversation with the woman next to me. I was asking her what she was doing. She answered that she was retired, and for fun she was running at the Senior Olympics. What? Olympics for seniors? Oh my goodness, I had another chance to participate!

I was ecstatic. I googled running magazines, I subscribed to one and I was all exited. I shared the story with people and…nothing. I still had to go through a lot of learning and digging up all the dirt, which was still lodged in my mind, my brain and every cell of my body until I was ready to take this on. Another three years of workshops, seminars and private help sessions went by until it hit me like a lightning bolt that I ***had*** to run.

In February 2007 I drove to Hollywood, and while I was on Wilshire Boulevard I asked myself, "What is it that I have to do in my life?" Not with my life – ***in*** my life. The answer came almost instantly. ***Sprint!*** Wow! I went home that evening and spoke with one of the tenants in the building where I live. She was a runner and a coach, and she offered to coach me. I was thrilled, to say the least. I had a coach; I felt like a pro!

The first time we went to the park, she asked me to do lunges. But I discovered that I couldn't pick up from 1959 and do what I did then. I ached, I hurt. My big toe was bloody, and I lost my toenail. Why? Because I didn't tell my coach that my toe was hitting the front of my running shoe. After that, I wasn't even able to jog for four months. I realized that this was another chance to jeopardize my training. When I practiced HapKiDo in New York from 1990 through 1993, I also pushed myself, hurt myself and wasn't able to continue. I had no goal then; there was no prize and I always told myself that nothing was going to happen anyway, so why continue?

This was different, though. This time I was not going to give up. I started with stretching, and I learned to be gentle and not push myself to the point of hurting. My coach always asked me how I was doing, and I needed an entire year to understand what I had to do, how I had to do it and what I had to be careful about not to do. I realized that all the workouts I had done for the past year had given me more strength. I was faster, I had more stamina and I believe that I had not reached my super duper speed and power yet!

I had another month and a half to train for the qualification race and I was nervous as can be, because I hadn't been on the track yet. Every time I was supposed to run, something happened. Either the track was down for repair, my coach had to fly off to another country, or my IT band was sore and she didn't want me to aggravate it any more. What is the IT band? The IllioTibial, or IT band is a thick piece of connective tissue that runs parallel to the femur from the hip to the knee. When your pelvis moves into an unfavorable position, the IT band pulls away from the knee, and it hurts really bad.

I was doing all the workouts my coach told me to do, from stretching, running up the steps in Santa Monica to the dunes in Manhattan Beach and even hiking in the Santa Monica Mountains.

My coach suggested that I keep a journal and write about everything I did and what I experienced. What I was accomplishing and how I felt and what I ate and what I thought and what I would like to happen. The best thing was that my Father was not behind me and threatening to open my diary, read it and then beat me again for writing about my dreams, my wishes and especially, the truth. I was going to do what I'd dreamed about and didn't do before. One thing I already knew, this was not going to be easy. But then, what is?

I was not sure if I was prepared to do what it would take; I only knew one thing for sure, I will give it my best.

My Journal

April 13, 2008

After waking up at around 4 am, I was happy that I had another two hours to sleep. Of course, I didn't fall asleep for another hour, and then at 6 am the alarm went off. It felt like it was screaming into my ear, and I jolted out of bed.

My cat was calling for food, so I fed him. Then I went into the living room and started my daily routine of loosening my wrists, then my elbow joints and then my shoulders. For 55 minutes I stretched, then did 40 crunches and 40 push-ups. During the exercise the idea of putting together a DVD for older women who want to work out at home popped up, and I thought it would be great.

Thoughts of what I was going to do to attract more clients in real estate entered my mind, and I stored them away. Right now I really only want to concentrate on what I have to do and not what I fear may happen. I want to eliminate those dark visions of the past. This has to be about now and how I am dealing with my daily life during this coming year and a half to make me realize that whatever I wish for in my life, somehow I ***can*** make it happen.

By 7:45 am I was finished with my shower, make-up and dressing. I got into my car and went to work at the real estate office, where I was helping out for one of our transaction coordinators, who had to take leave of absence for three months. Since I work every day Monday through Friday from 8 am or a little later until 6 pm, this will be challenging. Never mind, I am going to think positive. I am sure I am not the only person who is having challenges. Tomorrow is another day, and I have more training to do than just in the morning. I am keeping my fingers crossed, that I will manage.

April 26, 2008

Holy Moses! An entire week has gone by, and I was not able to write at all for a few days. What did I promise my coach? That I am going to write every day? Well, I didn't. Again, I am beating myself up for no reason. I trained every day, though. Every single day of the week I got up at 6 am and got one hour of training under my belt. One thing I realized when I was running twice this week, that my legs felt like lead. It will be interesting to hear what my coach has to say when I tell her tomorrow. Getting closer to the qualification race makes me understand that training for one hour a day and then working nine to ten hours will not get me to a win in any race. I have to start making concessions and eliminate certain activities and train more. What am I thinking? What other activities do I have? I am at work at 8 am – ah, maybe I run during my lunch hour – I leave the office at 6 pm and go home to take care of the building I live in and manage. Sometimes there is nothing at all to take care of, and I have time for myself. Other times, I have to check on stoves or toilets or open the door for people who lock themselves out. At the end of the month it is a little busier with rent roll, ordering supplies, and making phone calls to organize all the workmen for an empty apartment that has to get ready for the next tenant.

While writing this, I am thinking that the best way to get more organized is to make a schedule like I did in school and stick with it. One hour of training, work, running, work, building, workout and, after that, free time – whatever is left of the day. Ideas are tumbling through my head of having meetings with people who I want to approach to sponsor me. I also want to finish writing one of my other books. I would like to see friends from time to time. How do I fit in prospecting for real estate right now? Oh, I want a daddy, someone who takes care of me and helps me to make my wish come true. And by that, I mean a father, one I never had. I am smiling at myself; the daddy I want would have to be extremely old to be my father. In actuality I want to time travel, be 16 and have a father who supports me in my athletic career.

April 27, 2008

Today was a very important day for me, because I learned several things. My coach and I met at the Manhattan Beach dunes, and it was so hot I felt like I was in a pizza oven. I did some warm-up exercises and jogging and then some sprints. After that we went to the sand dune, and my coach told me that we are going to go up there four times. I thought I'd drop right there and then.

After taking off my shoes, I realized how hot the sand was, so I left my socks on. OK, off we went. The first third or maybe even less was OK, but then all of a sudden I had to take a rest. Then I went a little further and stopped, panting and getting really hot. I think I stopped another two times before I reached the top. My coach told me how well I did. I went by her to walk off the wobbly legs, and then I started crying, because I knew I would have to make the dune another few times. I was so angry at myself that I wasn't stronger. *OK, stop beating yourself up. You did fine. It's hot!* I always find a reason why I am not better; always, always making me feel smaller. I walked back to my coach, who said that we were done, it's too hot. Of course I apologized for not being able to do the dune again, and she told me that I did fine, and it was too hot to do it again.

At the bottom I drank some water. My coach asked me how much water I was normally drinking, and I told her about one to two small bottles a day. She very sternly told me that I had to drink at least ten bottles of water a day. Realizing how dehydrated I was, I understood that if I was not drinking any more water than I did, I would not be able to run in this heat. It will be hot at the games. It will be even hotter on the track.

Besides all of that, I made a very interesting discovery: I have to train how to start, how to get out of the blocks. Oh my goodness, I felt so silly not being able to do it right now. Another reason to be nervous. Again, I had to tell myself that everything will be all right, as long as I will practice. I practice everything else, so why shouldn't I get better every time I do it? I will! I know in my heart that I will get better. Lactic acid is making my legs feel like lead – great!

So it's 2:45 pm on Sunday. I am sitting at an Open House waiting for people to show up and buy the house. Oh, I am on my 5th bottle of water. Driving home from the training I was dripping wet. I had to take a shower and wash my hair, then I had a couple of eggs with salt and paprika and two pieces of pumpernickel bread and water. I had a short talk with my Hap-KiDo teacher in New York, who suggested making lemonade, adding agave juice and salt and drinking that, which will be my drink of choice tonight. Right now I am munching on an organic energy bar, and I hope that this will be enough until 5 pm when I close the door. Dinner tonight will be fish, and I'll go to sleep early.

I am determined to get up a little earlier tomorrow and run before I do my stretching routine. The letters are waiting to be sent to prospective sponsors. Financial support would really be great to afford the coach and physical therapy and massage therapy. Dreams and ideas are flooding my head. Again I am catching myself getting lost in too much dreaming. I want to focus on what is important, and that is where I am right now in this moment in time, who I am, what I want to accomplish and how I am realistically going to do it.

April 30, 2008

The alarm scared the living daylight out of me, and while I was laying there I thought how great it would feel to stay in bed for another few hours. I got up, brushed my teeth, fed the cat and exercised. Today is the last day of the month, and I practiced every morning, which makes me proud.

Yesterday evening I had an energy healing, and all of a sudden I can feel how I fill my lungs with air. Before, I never was able to go further than to my belly and then I stopped breathing in. Don't ask me why, I just did. This will make a tremendous difference when I am running. I can't wait until tomorrow morning when I go to the park.

I am surprised and then I really am not – because I expect so much from myself – that I didn't feel any pain after my treacherous walk up the sand dune in Manhattan Beach on Sunday.

Yesterday I signed up as a member of the Pasadena Senior Center, and I printed out the application for the 2009 Masters.

I want to go over it with my coach to remember everything I have to do. June 7, 2008, is the qualification race in Pasadena, and I am more confident, because I know I will be able to clock a time that allows me to qualify.

So now, for this coming month, it is health, health, health and more health. Asking all my friends and coworkers to remind me if they see me slip will help me to get me into perfect shape.

May 1, 2008

As usual, I got up at 6 am and went to the park. I jogged six rounds, and then I did four strides. This reminded me that I will have to take a tape measure next time I go to the park to find out how many feet – or better, how many yards – I run.

After I was done with my training, I went home and did my entire routine of stretching, sit-ups and push-ups, my stomach strengthening exercise. I also rolled my upper thighs on my foam roller. Boy, that hurt! While I was stretching I had a thought about my father for a split second. It was just enough to tell myself, *This is enough, I don't need to go there anymore*, and he disappeared for now.

Nothing out of the ordinary, just another day at work from 9 am – 6 pm.

The thought of training some more got me really excited and put a big smile on my face.

May 2, 2008

This morning I took the stairs to the gym and worked the treadmill. I ran for a while, and then I did three minutes on the highest incline; two minutes straight and another two minutes on the incline. After that I did leg weights and a few weights for my arms, following with my entire stretching routine, the usual push-ups, sit-ups and stomach strengthening exercise.

I worked in the office until 5 pm, then went home to prepare a little something for two film makers, who were coming over to discuss the possibility of a documentary.

The ladies arrived, and we had tea and apple strudel, which I secretly bought at the Swiss bakery. We shared stories from Austria and France, and we had a very nice conversation about when to begin filming. They were interested in following me to the various training places until next year when I participate in the National Games. It sounded very exciting. We made a plan for them to come to my first competition in Pasadena, and after that continue on.

May 3, 2008

As per my coach, I am taking the day off and treating myself to a reflexology massage, which I desperately need. So many thoughts are cramming my head. While driving to the Chinese massage place, I prepared myself to let go and allow myself to release the stress and enjoy my massage.

The darkened room almost immediately provided the space for me to let go of the worries and concerns. The masseuse ushered me to a bed. After my feet were gently placed into a bucket of warm water, tears found their way down my cheeks, and my body relaxed.

May 4, 2008

Finally I am on the track at UCLA! Ran three rounds and then did a little warm down. My coach had me running the straight sides and jogging the curves, after which I sprinted. Unfortunately, I didn't warm up enough, so I wasn't able to give it my all. How stupid of me! What the heck was I thinking? Obviously, nothing. So right after training, I drove home and had a smoothie. I needed to drive to the Valley for some business, so I took four ice packs and placed them on my thighs while I was driving.

After I was done with work, I took the time to relax and lounge around until I went to bed at 8:30 pm. Cringing about the fact that I need more rest now, this was yet another way to beat myself up. It was hard to stop thinking about being punished for being unable to go, go, go, not stopping ever. Then I paused in the middle of the thoughts, realizing that I am not made of steel. I am a human being.

May 5, 2008

Up at 5:30 am. Brushed my teeth, fed the cat and started with my routine. Yesterday my coach showed me a double skip, and I couldn't figure out how to do that. I felt like a fool. *Gee, how could I not get it?* This morning while preparing breakfast I practiced that double skip in the kitchen, and finally, I got it. I feel great, with no pain while stretching or walking up and down the stairs, so hopefully I didn't injure myself. Next time when I run, I definitely will warm up better than yesterday.

My thoughts took me back to 1959 when I was on the track running, jumping, playing around. I never had an issue with warming up too little. I didn't even know about warming up and stretching. Definitely different times now, and of course my body is demanding attention and definitely needs TLC. I really never waste any time or energy on thinking about the fact that I am older. I don't feel it, and I am telling myself that these little aches and pains are because I am not used to training. Of course I am fooling myself, because age does make a difference in my body and performance, especially after not doing that kind of strenuous training for so many years. Maybe I can cheat and perform miracles. Not really.

May 8, 2008

This morning I got up at 5:30 am, and after I took care of checking my email for the building, I walked over to the park. The hum from the cars on the 405 freeway seemed a little louder. The first person I saw was the grounds keeper in the park. He was putting ties on some large plastic bags filled with debris. I walked toward my trail, and nobody else was there. Not one single person. The ground was a little damp from the morning dew, and the park seemed wider than normal. I started jogging, and for my first round I didn't even see the usual dogs running around. No basketball players, not even the yoga people were there. I had the park completely to myself. Second round – aahh, one dog and his master. I ran along, and by the third round people were slowly populating the park. It had been nice having the park all to myself for a while.

While I was jogging, so many other things popped into my head, other than just my training routine.

It's a little difficult for me to write about what is going on in my life besides my training. There is stress, a lot of stress, which I have learned to hide – or better, ignore; nevertheless it is still there.

The thought of maybe getting out of real estate altogether and doing something completely different; and then, will that different ***thing be*** different? Explaining to the IRS why there was no positive income in my interior design business will be interesting. It was yet another failed attempt to make it work. I guess my worries are not any different than anyone else. It's all good! I know it will be, but the question remains: when? Right now, that thought is being pushed aside.

May 10, 2008

I got up at 6 am, brushed my teeth, went downstairs, got in the car and drove to UCLA to get on the track. I turned into the parking structure and looked down onto the track and could not believe my eyes. People in dark green uniforms with back packs were jogging around the track. I stopped the car and stared. On the side I saw someone else stretching – now mind you, it was Saturday at 6:30 in the morning, and people were already training . I was so mad. No, it was more a feeling of disappointment and fear. How could I go down there? *I can't! I am embarrassed.* The track was swarming with people. I was by myself and without my coach, who was in San Francisco, and I couldn't get on the track. Oh, how my mind was playing tricks on me. I turned around and drove back home, parked my car in the garage and hit my steering wheel. How could I allow myself to become this fearful and run away? I quietly cried, shook my head in disbelief, got out of the car and went to the park.

It was pretty empty still, only a handful of people were with their dogs and playing in the grass. I started jogging, did my six rounds, felt really great and continued to do my stretching, my leg exercises, which look like As and Bs, etc. I stretched my upper thighs and didn't feel any pain. Then I started running, this time a little faster: first 50 meters, maybe it was a little more, a little less. Still fine, then a second time a little faster, still OK. Third time I felt a little twinge in my hip flexor, so I walked back – no, I jogged back to where I started and stretched my legs. I prepared myself to run 100 meters.

OK. I stood there, concentrated and bang – off I went, and I sprinted. Well, after a few seconds I felt it in my IT band. And yes, I finished, but I knew I was not able to do the second 100 meters. Anger was again coming up in me. I walked back and thought, *Well, maybe I try*. I should have remembered what my martial arts master said to me years ago: *Trying is failing, just do it!*

I started, and after a few steps I knew I had to let go and stop. I jogged so I would not injure myself more. I jogged for a few minutes, and then I walked home. For the life of it, I didn't understand what had happened. Why now? Why now?

I am always asking the same questions. *Why is this happening? What is the reason?* And who knows how many more questions that make me believe I am not worth it, it won't happen, I do not amount to anything...and on and on and on.

In the afternoon I drove to Irvine to see my friend, whom I hadn't seen in two years. She is a Black Belt in HapKiDo, she rode her mountain bike from Russia to China and she is a superstar! Another one of her friends, who coaches her, came by later. We discussed my pains, and she asked me if I'd changed my diet. I didn't think so.

On my way home that night, I still was thinking about why I would hurt myself now. My mind took me back to the morning, and the question arose about why I was not able to go down to the track. Why was I so scared that people would look at me and not allow me to train? I had slipped back into being 16 years old and afraid of my Dad. Of course, right now I felt pathetic, and I realized that situations like this one would come up. I needed to work on getting more confidence and realizing that not everything I do will be wrong, or what seemed to be wrong in my Father's eyes. I want to face my fear, stare it down and make it as small as dust.

May 11, 2008

In the morning, after a long and restful sleep, I had this idea: I trained all these months on grass. I sprinted on grass. During the last two weeks, I started in the park on cement. Then, last week on the track, where I hurt, and yesterday in the park on cement again. I believe that may be the culprit. I changed something in my training, and maybe the cement did it to me. Then it hit me, The fear made my body stiff, and that's how I hurt myself.

Tomorrow I will go to the Joint Rehabilitation Center. It's not for something I've smoked. It's for the joints in my body. I'll ask them to look at my legs and find out what I have to do to heal quickly. I have only four more weeks until the qualification race, and I want to be ready to run and not wait another two years. God help me ***please***!

Of course, I realize that nothing is doing this to me. I am doing it to myself. Nobody is beating me up anymore! Why is it that I am clinging to that awful need of feeling pain? Emotional, physical, psychological pain; it seems like I am looking for it.

May 14, 2008

The last three days went by in a whirlwind, and I don't know where to begin. I guess I'll start at the beginning.

Monday – oh yes, Monday! I got up and did my exercises as usual; I was really happy that I didn't hurt too much. Yes, I felt my IT band, gosh was I ticked off! Anyway, I called one of my friends, who is a producer, and we finally made an appointment to meet on Tuesday at 10 am to discuss the possibilities of some kind of sponsorship. The day went by without any major glitches, and I was thinking how great it would feel if I could take off from work and train. Oh yes, it would be nice to have the luxury of not working.

Tuesday I got up, exercised, stretched a lot and went to work very early. Then I drove to Hollywood for my meeting.

Very interesting, ***very*** interesting! This was my first business meeting for myself, and I learned a lot. Not everything was about my running. A little small talk, a little fun, and in between questions; I mentioned that someone was interested in making a documentary. And of course, because I am not familiar with film work and production, etc., I offered to get all the people together. This was going to be more than one or two meetings. It would depend on what everybody wants to give, and what they would like to get out of it, and I am going with the flow.

Tuesday evening I had dinner with clients, who opened my eyes to possibilities about what I could do on the internet. That also involves other people and more meetings and finding out about each other and getting a partner. I am really very excited and even though nothing has been resolved or accomplished, the ball started to roll. I feel that something interesting is in the making.

Today I raced through my routine, except for the stretching and taking care of the pain with my IT band. Wednesday next week I have an appointment with the doctor at the Joint Rehabilitation Center, and by then I should be feeling better. This weekend I will be sprinting, so I am taking it really easy and not running at all until then.

Tonight I am having another meeting with yet someone else about some interior design business. The young woman was asking me to help her buying the perfect furniture for her new apartment. I will do the best I can. I have come to the definite conclusion that my life as a real estate agent is going to continue, and I am not going to do something else. Even though the market is going through a dry spell right now and sales are down, I cannot imagine sitting in an office every single day from 9 to 5. Real estate is giving me enough freedom to take care of business, managing the building, training and even doing some interior design. I just have to divide my time slots properly.

May 15, 2008

I fell into bed at around 11 pm last night, rolled out of it after a deep and dreamless sleep by 6 am and did my exercises. All these thoughts about what's going on in my life wrecked my concentration and affected what I had to do to stay focused, balanced and grounded. I realized that I didn't ground myself before I started. What a difference it makes!

I prayed that something will open up, like the heavens, and I will receive an answer on what I should do and how to get rid those voices in my head. For the life of it, I do everything I am supposed to do, thinking positive and saying ***"stop"*** if something negative comes up. My affirmations, my prayers, my gratitude prayers and the thought that I am making it, didn't help at all. I have a vision wall. Not just a board, an entire wall. Sometimes I even dream of my success. I know in my heart that I am supposed to be in a different situation but still – ***nothing***! I watched the movie "The Secret", in which experts are talking about what to do to change your attitude, hoping to learn how to attract everything positive in my life. I read books after that, and then some people tell me the reason why nothing changes in my life is because I do not believe I deserve to be in a better place. Hearing that makes me angry. I know I deserve to be happy, healthy and wealthy.

Yes, I am surrounded by wonderful friends who are supporting me right now, and I truly appreciate that. I wouldn't know what to do without them. This is completely crazy, and I will have to meditate on that to find an answer. Because if I continue to be stressed, I can't train. And no training, no Olympics; and that's out of the question. That's an absolute ***no***!

May 18, 2008

I took off today. I did my gardening, and then I had to work a little; yet another side job – organizing people's offices and homes. I can't wait for Wednesday when I will find out what is happening to my IT band and what they have to do to fix it.

I woke up this morning at 6:15, and then I decided to stay in bed a little longer. I had the wildest dreams. They were completely sexual, and I have no clue what to make of it other than maybe I should open myself to be with a man again…that's scary. I have to think about that for a while before I jump into it***…hahaha.***

Anyway, someone may be out there waiting to love me, and I am not aware of it other than in my dreams. It will be interesting to find out who it is. I received a letter yesterday, which I only picked up from my mailbox this evening. I always wait until the weekend is over to get my mail from Saturday. I was wondering what someone from the Austrian American Council West would want from me. OMG - a gentleman sent a check for $1,000 with a note explaining that he wanted to help me through my training. I was floored, surprised and happy. Yeah – thank you!

May 21, 2008

OK, so I spent three hours at the Joint Rehabilitation Center to get my body put back together. First with the nurse to get blood pressure and answer general questions about where it hurts and when. Very nice lady.

Then I waited for a little while to see the doctor. Oh boy! He said it as it is: no strength in my right foot and ankle, motion in right leg less than in left one, hip needs to be adjusted, gluteus maximus needs strengthening, too. IT band is OK; and he asked me about my stress level, to which I answered 975 out of 1000. Adrenal glands are very low, too. So the summary is as follows: I need a complete overhaul, lube job, change of tires, motor wash and detailing. Just kidding. I told the doctor that my qualification race is June 7, and he said, "...and you are waiting until the 5th to see me?" I like his sense of humor.

They took some x-rays of my right hip to make sure nothing major is wrong with it. Then they did some ultrasound to warm up the muscles in my right leg and get them to loosen up. After that I went back to see the doctor. He taped my feet and instructed me to do several exercises, no running for two days (I haven't been running for over a week now anyway, not to aggravate whatever hurts any more) and to see him again on Friday.

On another note, I received an email from my former partner and friend in interior design. She offered me a small job, organizing a house for one of her clients, who just moved, and I accepted. That is going to be for the next few evenings, and then I'll finish it over the Memorial Day weekend. I am happy!

May 30, 2008

I went to physical therapy and had a long discussion with the doctor. He asked me if we had discussed my x-rays, and I answered, "No, should we?"

Of course we had to, and we went into the exam room, where he told me that he will make me a radiology expert in five minutes. LOL! He explained a regular chart to me, and then he showed me my own spine. OK, it looked great; everything was in perfect place and shape. I thought it was not so good, because what do I know? He told me it was perfect; and then he asked me if I saw one particular line. Of course I saw the line. What was it? My number five lumbar. Oops! It was completely disintegrated. Great! Tears welled up in my eyes, and I immediately had an anxiety attack – inside though, I couldn't let the doctor see that, right? Right!

The fear that I was not able to run was right in front of my eyes. I only heard, "Well, that is the reason why you feel the pain in your legs. You will be limited in your movements. That should be the worst that happens to you." Of course it was easy for him to say, he doesn't want to run the 100 meters in the Senior Olympics.

"So, can I run on June 7th?" The doctor was holding the chart and bobbing his head. I wanted to punch him.

"How far do you have to run?"

"It's only 100 meters, 16 seconds."

"So, when did you run 16 seconds the last time?"

"Well, my coach clocked me at 80 meters three weeks ago at 11.6 seconds."

"OK, we'll fix you."

After I left, I got into my car and screamed the blue from the sky. I cursed, I cried and I was consumed by fear that I would have to run in pain. I didn't even know what to think. In the office I was crying some more, and I spoke with some of my friends. Finally I got over it and said, "I don't give a hoot. I'll just run and that's that."

Of course it was mental; but there was a reality I had to deal with. My body is not perfect, and I have to make adjustments to be able to compete and win. So, here I was having a physical challenge, which I didn't expect. OK, let's deal with it.

It's the disc, which is disintegrated. Damn, you little sucker, where have you gone? Why do you have to do that to me? Just disappear from my spine and leave me? Well, I learned to deal with abandonment a long time ago, and I will deal with this one, too. I am so aware that I am living in my head, which makes me also realize that I am missing out on living in the now. My past still has me in its grip. "Oh boy!" Will this ever end? Of course, Dad kicking me with his boots and punching his fist into my back wouldn't have anything to do with it. It was there, right in front of me. It made me so mad.

June 5, 2008

Two days before the race! The past week has been extremely busy for me regarding business. I was working with two clients at the time, juggling one appointment with the next, besides having to be in the real estate office taking care of administrative stuff and getting ten apartments rented in the building I manage, which I set out to do before I leave for Europe at the end of July.

It looks like all the apartments are rented, and I got one client into a condo for six months. Maybe by the end of the day I will find a place for the martial arts master. I almost finished the job organizing the files for another client. Of course, I will have more room to breathe after the race on Saturday. Gee, it couldn't have happened before? I am really grateful about all this activity – I mean, I asked for it. It's just that it never happens the way we imagine. Another lesson to learn for me is to accept and stop complaining.

I visited the Joint Rehabilitation Center almost every second day to get my body back into shape. Not that I was out of shape, it just needed adjustments and help from a professional to stretch a little more and get to know my body better. From last Friday until today, the doctor also changed the tune of his voice, and now he tells me that I will do a phenomenal job! I guess he wanted me to be aware of what is going on inside of me and take care of it properly.

Tonight I am going to go to the UCLA track to jog around the block – or the track, so to speak – and put on my spikes for the first time. At least I will know what it feels like to get out of the blocks and run in spikes. I am a little nervous – of course, what else is new? I haven't done this in almost 50 years, so I invited my friend to come with me. That is how chicken I am to go somewhere by myself for the first time. Oh boy, this is so silly. But I feel better and more secure having someone with me, in case they ask me why I am there, etc. Still needing emotional support!

My friend and I discussed this, and I said to her that I have the perfect answer if someone asks me if I am attending classes at UCLA. Why not tell them I was at UCLA in 1902, and at that time we were having class in someone's kitchen and only had one subject: making chicken soup? Hahaha, always ready to make a joke!

Well, we shall see. Maybe there won't be anyone there – hopefully, so I can concentrate on what I have to do, or all this preparation may be for the birds.

So many worries, so many concerns, so many voices in my head and all the ups and downs I am going through. I wonder if other people have similar anxieties when they have to do something for the first time. I realize no matter how young or old I am, something is going to happen in my life where I am a little rattled. OK, that too shall pass, and I know I will be fantabulous! See you at the finish line.

June 6, 2008

Yesterday at the track, my friend came with me. Of course other people were on the track doing their own stuff and

nobody bothered with me. It was great, and I felt relieved, so next time I can do this alone. I did my warm-up, jogging, ran up and down the stairs and then sprinted. My friend made the comment that I am too fast for her to count. Funny girl!

Today I took the day off. After the doctor visit, I went briefly to the office and then drove to the Pasadena Senior Center to pick up my stuff, so I have one less thing to think about tomorrow. I made this an easy day, but of course there had to be a glitch with one of my clients. I had to make an emergency call to have their unit cleaned tomorrow. I was at the doctor three times this week and had all kind of rehabilitation treatments, and I truly hope that tomorrow everything will fall into place, and I will be able to run without pain.

The week went by so quickly, and if I was wrapped any tighter I probably would snap. So I am going to bed now and will get up in the morning and see where I am at and what I am going to do.

Let the Games Begin

June 7, 2008

Well, it's all over now, and here it is what happened.

I got up at 6 am. I did my stretching routine, sit-ups, push-ups and the rest of my preparation work. When I was ready to take my shower, my phone rang, and I had to take care of some business. So before I went to Pasadena, I had to make sure that everything was OK for my client, and then I turned my phone off. I didn't want to hear anything anymore; I wanted to relax – if that was even possible – and prepare myself for the track meet.

Of course, I was early. What else is new? There was nothing for me to do other than to walk around and then find a place where I was able to warm up. I had about 2-1/2 hours. What to do? I was sitting, walking, sitting again, walking around, and then I started to warm up. I jogged a little after stretching, and then I sprinted. I felt the pain in my IT band. Damn it! So I went to the bathroom and put some soothing gel on the leg, went back to my little secret area and sprinted again. More pain! I went back to the bathroom, more gel, two pain patches and then back to prepare; still painful. OK! I stopped, went to the track and realized how wired I was. The only thing I was thinking was, *What if the pain is soooo bad that I can't run? What the heck am I going to do? I was training all this time and then I fail?* I was stressed out, so I ate a power bar, went to the first aid area and found a table where they had some bananas. I took two and stuffed them into my mouth, then I walked around again. Oh my goodness! What am I going to do?

I went over to the starting area and asked the gentleman when he would be calling us. He told me that they were a little behind and it would be after the men's 800 meter. Then I saw my friend, and she took my mind off the race. Some other friends joined, and I paced back and forth some more. Finally we were called, and I was able to get on the track, pick up the blocks and get into them. What a disaster! I had no clue how to adjust them, so I was uncomfortable. I didn't know what height would be perfect for me. Now that stressed me out! So I decided to chuck the blocks. I remembered that my coach had said to me, "If you are not using the blocks, do not get on the ground. Just go low, but do not get on the ground to start."

I tried that and my leg hurt, so I thought, *I cannot do that. I will not be able to get off in time with that pain.* Then I saw the woman on my left on the ground without the blocks and I said to myself, *Screw that, I am getting on the ground and that's that.*

I walked a little back and forth, and then I focused on the track – on my lane. Lane #3.

Then it was time to start. I crouched down, listened to the gunman and followed his voice. The gun went off, and I was off. And this is what happened:

I started running and, *oh no, two women on my right are in front of me. Oh my gosh, why can't I run faster? Why are my legs like lead? Oh my, let me run faster.* And then it was over. At 17.37

seconds, I came in third, and I qualified.

I ran past the finish line. That's when I broke down and started crying and crying and crying. I realized I did it. I finally did it. After 49 years, I was in a competition and qualified. Of course, immediately after I heard my time, I started to beat myself up, that I didn't run faster, that I wasn't able to run the 100 meters in 14 seconds. My friend consoled me, and then I realized that this had been my first 100 meters in almost 50 years. And damn it, it was good. And – no pain! At the moment I thought of it, it amazed me that I had no pain. Where did it disappear to? Magic – poof – gone!

The producer and the cameraman who are making the documentary took the time to interview me for quite a while. After thanking my friends for their support and cooling down I went to my favorite Chinese woman to have my legs massaged. I felt no pain running, no pain at all, and I was fine. All that tension I had stored in my body was gone. What a relief!

I am fine, now I can focus on my speed and concentrate to get faster. I have an entire year to shave off at least three seconds to have a chance of winning a medal. God willing and taking care of my body, it will happen.

Thank you, Universe, for right now; thank you!

CA Games – Pasadena 2008

Ingrid Kern

has qualified for the 2009 National Senior Games
by placement or minimum performance standard
in the following events:

Track and Field - 100M

We'll see you in Palo Alto
August 1–15, 2009

June 12, 2008

It has been almost a week ago since I qualified for next year's games, and I have seen the doctor twice this week. Today I had my blood drawn to see what my body needs and what is lacking regarding supplements and all the other good stuff. Even though I am taking customized supplements, I believe something is missing in my body, because my fingernails are the pits right now. They are breaking and peeling, never mind that I always had the strongest nails before. We shall find out!

I have been doing my stretching routine, and next week I start running again. Funny, the doctor said today, "There is some stress in your body."

My answer to that was, "Duh!" I went to the bank today to deposit some checks and saw my balance. The thoughts that went through my head were, *Gee, I am working my behind off. But because I am not receiving any money for showing properties and not selling, my money is not growing. It's getting less while I am watching. Of course I am stressed! How am I going to be able to relax and focus on my training? Something has to break, something has to give. This is too much. I can't take this anymore. I want to be able to live stress-free and train and write and stop worrying. I am not going to take this anymore. I have enough. This is it. I want to work less and make more money.*

I shook my head in disbelief. If I only could shut those voices down, I'd be all right, because in truth I am all right. I have everything I need, and then some. I am able to train and write, and all I need to do is stop worrying. I promise that to myself. Unfortunately, it is so easy to slip into the mode of feeling threatened and not being taken care of; still such a familiar feeling. How terrible! Writing about it makes me see the craziness of it all. The question arises, would it be easier with someone at my side to comfort me?

June 19, 2008

It has been 12 days since I sprinted into qualification, and it has been quiet. Quiet in the respect of training! I have not been running at all to relax and calm down from all the excitement before the race. I have been doing my daily stretching routine and the usual push-ups, sit-ups and weight training, but no running. I have seen the doctor a few times, and today I received a scolding – only verbally – for eating too much sugar. OK, so today I am making a vow: I am cutting down on my intake of sweets altogether. I realize now that if I eat a lot of sugar, then I feel weak the next day. It's something I never realized before – well, I mean, before I started training.

Work has been bland, to put it mildly. I am in the middle of closing a lease outside of the building I manage, and one of my clients wants to buy a home and is very busy right now, so we play a waiting game.

Learning to be patient is extremely difficult for me, because if I am not doing something all the time, I feel I am not accomplishing anything. Again, I have this feeling of being useless. Thanks, Dad.

I can't wait to get the pictures from the photo shoot. Then I will send out some letters for sponsorship next week. It will be interesting to see how that is going to work out. I am confident that something good is happening, and it all will turn out fabulous.

July 4, 2008

Listening to the distant fireworks at 9 pm while I am sitting in front of my computer – alone. What does that tell me about myself? How does it feel right now, and how do I handle being by myself? Working all the time, training and being alone, that's my life.

It only hits me when I have time on my hands, like today. Normally after I am done working in the real estate office, I come home, work some more at the building, probably work on the computer, eat dinner and go to sleep. In the morning I get up, exercise, and go to work and then the same routine.

Now I have three days on my hands, and I am sure tomorrow I will be busy working at the building. Tonight though, I am alone. Yes, I am emotional about that, and I would love to be with someone right now. Hmm. So yes, sacrifices need to be made when one has a goal, and I do have one; a big one! I need to be by myself for the coming year to be able to concentrate on my training and get better and better to have a chance of winning a medal.

In the meantime, I do have dreams and imagine being with a man, someone who will be waiting for me at the finish line and sweep me off my feet. I truly feel like a little kid dreaming of something fabulous to happen in my life; and I guess it will! Happy 4th of July! I'm in the mood for love.

Life Is Happening

August 21, 2008

A lot has happened since I last wrote in my journal, and on the other hand not a lot has changed. I flew to Vienna at the end of July to spend some time with my nephew, who was getting married. The computer stayed home. I knew before I left that this trip would be different than all the others before. I felt that I was ready to make peace with my father by visiting his grave. I've done all this work on getting to the place where I am today. I've made a step to be at peace with him emotionally and spiritually, but I was never able to visit his grave and feel at peace. I also knew that this would be the last time in my life to be staying in the same apartment where I grew up and look at it from a completely different point of view.

First, two fabulous days in London with my very dear friend before I flew off to Vienna gave me time to adjust from work to a little freedom and vacation. I continued to exercise in the morning before we had breakfast, after which we took the tube into the city. A little shopping, lots of people watching and a little caviar and champagne in the afternoon at Harrods. My friend had arranged for a masseuse to come to the house and pamper us. In the evening a few of her friends came over, and we had a sumptuous dinner. Exchanging stories, having lots of fun with my friend made the time fly by, and then it was off to Austria.

My nephew and his future bride picked me up at the airport, and we drove to the apartment, which I called home for so many years. Nothing had really changed. The apartment was still dark. It seemed as if dampness was crawling into my bones. Signs of water intrusion from the upstairs apartment were on the kitchen ceiling, and I felt like taking a trip back into the past. Only this time, I was watching myself looking at everything. Looking at my nephew's belonging strewn everywhere, I realized right in front of me was my emotional chaos I went through during all those years. *I saw my mother sitting at the kitchen table doing her crossword puzzle. I got lost in my thoughts and stared at the window. My sister opened the door behind me and her voice made me turn.* Suddenly I was present to being alone in the apartment.

It seemed like it all happened yesterday, and yet I felt nothing; it was like I was watching a movie internally, and I observed everyone involved including myself. At that point I knew I was done. I'd finished that chapter of my life. I had nothing else to do, nowhere else to look or to dig. It was over, or so I thought. How wrong it proved to be.

The only thing left was to go to the cemetery. My nephew took me to my father's grave, where he lit a candle. Handing it to me he said, "I am leaving you alone now." I took the candle, bent down and put it into the small area next to the head stone. At that moment I started choking, and tears welled up in my eyes. Right then I heard my father's voice, speaking to me in German. "Now stop that whining already." He used a very unusual Viennese word for crying, which I haven't thought of in who knows how many years. It made me smile, and I knew we were all right. I walked to the front of the grave, sat down and touched the flowers. I said, "OK, Dad. Now we are done. I love you." I walked away and didn't look back once.

The two weeks in Vienna went by so quickly. The first evening I spent with the bride and her bridesmaids in a quaint restaurant. The next morning we drove to the castle where my nephew's wedding took place. Oh my, what a place. A small castle, not like the one I once stayed at in Salzburg. But what a little treasure box. The owners greeted us on the steps to the second floor with a smile on their faces that could melt a glacier. Everyone received a small bouquet of wild flowers, and then we were ushered to our individual rooms. It was like stepping back in time, being enveloped in history. There was not much time to get lost in thoughts. We had to get ready for an early lunch, after which we got dressed for the wedding.

The bride was gorgeous in her white gown, and the groom looked really handsome. The ceremony made me feel very emotional, and I had to hold back a few tears. Dinner was scrumptious, and we celebrated and danced into the night.

Way after midnight everyone went to their rooms, and I dreamed of my prince. Why not? I was in a castle. The next morning, after breakfast, we drove back to Vienna. I met with some of my cousins and also had enough time to visit with a few of my old friends. It was like going from breakfast to lunch to dinner for almost all the time. Everybody wanted to feed me and hear about Los Angeles. I had but two days by myself, which I used to walk through the center of the city. How beautiful the old buildings were! I was tempted a few times to say something out loud, which would have made me look really silly, so I smiled and admired the architecture. Then I was ready to fly back home to Los Angeles. Even though Vienna is a beautiful city, I don't feel that I am connected to it or that I belong there.

On the way to the airport my nephew and I exchanged a few stories about my mother and commented how we all missed her. He thanked me for the wedding gift, and he promised to open it after he got home. We gave each other a long embrace as if we both knew that it probably would be a long time before I would return to Vienna.

Now it is back to business and training again. It was an amazing experience for me to come back this time. I haven't been on a vacation for more than a few days in a very long time, and all the issues and challenges that I left behind before I went on this trip smacked me right in my face. Wow! I have to take care of a lot of stuff and yes, there are challenges to be met and overcome. I will write about them, and hopefully, I will be able to shed light on what has been hidden and things will change. I know they will, because I refuse to live in fear again.

Working on my other book, finding the right cover for the title page, getting it ready to be published. By the time this one is published, *What's Your Monster's Name?* has probably been available for a while. I am also taking care of my clients and business in general, getting letters out to prospective sponsors.

In the meantime, I have been watching the Olympic Games and am in awe of Usain Bolt. What an inspiration! Now I am going to be more intense than before, and I am going to do everything and anything to get my body, mind and spirit aligned to win a medal next August. For a moment I thought that this is an obsession – the thought that I have to win. I am going to sit with this for a while and look into this deeper. I am being driven by the thought of winning, not running and participating, no – winning. I wonder if I am going to miss out on something if I continue to feel this way.

August 25, 2008

Yesterday I was invited to a friend's afternoon party. Standing there, scanning the crowd with my eyes, I caught the face of a man standing across the room. I took a deep breath at first and turned the other way. I put down my glass, turned and walked toward the group of people where he was talking to my friend. I smiled, and before I knew it, he took my hand and introduced himself. After some small talk about business and Los Angeles, he asked if I would like to have dinner with him one evening. I gasped for air. Needless to say, I felt this incredible chemistry between us right away. I would have loved to throw all my doubts and concerns overboard and fling myself into his arms right there and then. What a thought!

Momentarily my head began to fill with thoughts and doubts. He is too this, and he is too that, and I am…and I am not…and that even if we would want to be with each other, my focus would shift. I started dreaming about how I want to spoil him, cook for him, take care of him and be with him and eventually would forget about ***me***! How would that work out for my goal to win the Masters next year? Not! I was so lost in my thoughts, when suddenly I felt a hand on my arm and a voice next to my ear, "Christian to Ingrid! Where are you? Are you listening to me?"

"Oh, I am so sorry that was really rude of me." I heard myself saying, and then I placed a kiss on his cheek.

He grabbed my arm, bent his head toward me and whispered in my ear, "Let's go someplace else."

Off we went without saying good-bye to anyone, at which point I thought that no one would miss us anyway. He took me by my hand. We ran to his car, and we drove to the beach. I felt like a little girl and giggled, and he laughed and his eyes smiled at me. He parked the car, and then we sat and stared into each other's eyes until one of us made a move toward the other. Then it all got dark, because I closed my eyes, and we kissed and kissed and kissed some more. Ecstasy!

OMG – what is going to happen? Where will this take me? Damn – I am always living in my head! Those thoughts were back again; I can't get away from them. Still not living in the ***now***! His soft voice reminded me that I am here, and I smiled at him. "Thank you!"

He said, "Thank you," while he pulled me even closer to caress me. We were sitting there intertwined, holding each other, kissing each other until he burst out laughing, "My goodness, that was quite something. I feel like a teenager."

I answered quietly, "I don't know what to say."

He put his finger on my lips and smiled. "Are you hungry?" I nodded. We decided to get something to eat and ended up in a restaurant right at the beach. After a cocktail and some food, we were blessed with the most incredible sunset. He asked about my life, and I told him a little bit about my journey. I hesitantly asked him if he was single, and he nodded yes. He told me that he was traveling a lot, having business in Chicago, and he hoped to see me again when he came back from his trip.

After a while Christian drove me back to my friend's house, where my car was parked. I thanked him, jumped into my car and raced off. I was too much into what happened to continue the party or talk to anyone.

That was seductive! Never mind, I have to keep my eye on the ball. My voices were right there again. At the same time I am battling with the desire, which is bursting inside my body, and it is in every one of my pores, thinking about being with a man. I am going to turn this feeling into speed and run like the wind; run with wings beneath my feet, run, and run, run.

September 6, 2008

I have been training the last week every single day again. And of course, after the first time jogging and doing weights, I hurt. My hip flexor muscles were telling me that I overdid it a little. I was hurting every time I got up after sitting for a while, and I felt like an invalid. Gee, why is this so difficult? Anyway, after the second day I was fine again. I jogged again, and this time I left the weights on the rack and did my stretching routine after running.

I also got in touch with my nutritionist and told him that I am literally jumping out of my skin. The skin on my right foot and on my left fingers is peeling like I am shedding my old skin. Thank goodness I was able to take care of it before my date tonight – how embarrassing that would have been. I don't even want to think about it! Nevertheless, I am stressed. In another week my coach is coming back from her honeymoon, and I do need to begin training with her again. I hope that I didn't do too much damage to my body.

I am working on publishing my other book. Oh dear God, life is a bowl of cherries. Sometimes you get a pit, and if you are lucky you won't chip a tooth.

September 7, 2008

Last night was a delight. Christian picked me up at my apartment. We went to Geoffrey's in Malibu. Dinner was scrumptious. The conversation was about to turn very personal when he asked me why I was so afraid of intimacy. Oh boy, that was a loaded question! I stopped chewing my food and froze. How was I going to answer without making him run for the hills?

"Hmm," I heard myself saying, and then nothing. For a few seconds we stared at each other. Then I said, "Well, I could tell you all about my entire life, but that probably would take a while. So I will tell you the short version. Right now I have a goal, and that is to compete at the Senior Olympics. It needs my complete attention, and everything else would take my attention away from it."

Christian looked at me and said, "Fair enough." Later, when we were quietly watching the sunset, he embraced me and whispered in my ear, "You're quite something."

The evening ended with him driving me home and a kiss good night in front of my building. Of course, I immediately doubted that I would ever see him again. I was not used to being with someone, who didn't argue with me about why I shouldn't do what I wanted to do.

September 29, 2008

Another month has gone by, and I have been fiercely struggling to meditate, getting into a positive frame of mind and let go, let go and let God. Everything is taking forever, the economy is lousy and my clients are frustrated. So am I! I have been training by myself. My coach is going to have a few words to say about that, and she also wants to make sure that I am having physical therapy to heal properly. I am taking it easy. I do my regular stretching routine, and I use the bike downstairs in my gym. I am on the treadmill too, but only to jog and run for a little while. No sprinting; otherwise, I am going to hurt myself again. Writing my thoughts, ideas and actions down makes me realize that I am constantly living in my head. ***Aya!*** I know this all shall pass, and I am going to be OK. I have written some letters to a few corporations asking for sponsorship. We'll see if someone will answer. It would be really nice to get some financial support. Of course, this is a long shot. If I don't attempt, I won't get, right?

Looking back on September, I have to admit that some very exciting things happened.

First, I was invited to be the guest at the John Solari Show, "The Method Actor Speaks," a half-hour local cable TV show. That was fun; the entire half hour was focused on me! We spoke about acting and modeling and real estate and writing and my running.

Then a photographer, whom I met at the Chris Howard seminar, sent me an email asking if I was interested in posing for some pictures for an Inner Vision poster. ***Yes***, of course I was interested. So we went to the track, and she took pictures of me running through the ribbon at the finish line – like the one at the end of a Marathon – with my book, *What's Your Monster's Name?* held high up in the air. The poster looks really nice, and I can't wait to have one in my office.

And then, of course, there is the new distraction from everything: Christian, whom I met a month ago. His life and business trips have been giving me the space I need. He is a very comforting, caring, and understanding and is a positive addition to my life. We see each other when he is in town, which has been only a couple of times since we met, and he inspired me to get away from the journaling and write something more romantic:

My Dream Home
Majestic palm trees sway in the evening summer breeze. The ever so slight shshsh sound of the fronds makes me look up and then I see the orange red fiery sun setting on the water. If it weren't for the waves gliding to the shore, the white crest of the crown slumping into the grains of sand on the beach, the sea – dark blue and glistening - looks almost still. For a moment I stand still, my skin warmed from the day in the sun, I stretch out my arms, close my eyes, and with a smile on my face, I say, "Thank you God, thank you God for the abundance in my life." I take another deep breath, open my eyes and continue the

walk to my house on the winding way strewn with white pebbles. "Ouch!" I am barefoot and one of the pebbles got caught between my little toe and the ring toe – that's what I call it. I bend down and slip into my pink tennis shoes, not even tying the laces. Still bent down to the ground, I lift my head to glance over the area to both sides of the house. A never- ending sea of soft green grass blankets the ground sprinkled with wildflowers in between the palms, which makes it look like a picture from a fairy tale.

I continue my walk to the front door of my home. It happens every time when I stand here, which is not so often, because normally I drive right into the adjacent garage and enter the hallway from there. I am in awe! This is my home! My architect breathed some Spanish into the Contemporary building by choosing a rather soft yellow gold color for the outside. He kept the structure to two stories high. Large picture windows on both sides of the door framed with the same wood as the door makes the house look very warm and inviting. The doors are made from magnificent brown red wood, and both doors have etched glass panels. On the left panel Poseidon, the God of the Sea, rules his side of the door and faces the other panel, on which one of the Sea Goddesses is seen sitting on a rock, her long hair flowing into the sea, her hand caressing a water lily. How lucky to have found this glass master, who put all his pride into finishing my doors.

I reach for the door handle, which glides into my hand like silk, and I open the massive door. Stepping into the entry, a light wind, coming through the opened French doors in the back of the house, makes it a little hard to keep the door from slamming. I turn around and close it gently. I take off my shoes to feel the cool marble under my feet. I immediately become aware of the beautiful sound of my favorite CD, "Songs of Awakening" with Lama Gyuerme's deep, rich voice chanting and Jean-Philippe Rykiel's keyboard. My French chef must be in heaven. That thought goes through my mind as, listening to this music, he definitely is preparing my favorite dish. "Bon soir, Michel!" I call out and quickly run up the open winding staircase to the second floor. On top of the stairs I turn toward the downstairs entry, leaning over the railing and call my housekeeper's name. WOW! I am hanging over the rail realizing I could fall two stories down and really hurt myself. Slowly I am pulling myself up.

My housekeeper is nowhere to be seen, and I make my way toward my bedroom. I want to quickly take a shower before I sit down for dinner. The double doors to my bedroom are open. I still can see part of the sun disappearing behind the ocean. I sneak a quick peek through the large window, my eyes getting caught on the soft green linen sheets gracing my king-size bed. I found the perfect 3-drawer set in an antique store in Spain, which I had shipped to me and I placed them on each side of the bed. A small ottoman with my evening attire laid out stands at the foot of my bed. I turn around to enter my bathroom. Again I smile at myself in sheer wonder that I am here. I made my bathroom an oasis where I can rest from the day's chores. I am surrounded by white walls, which gives the room a serene feeling. Chrome faucets at the green glass sinks and white marble on the floor. The glass closed-in shower with an enormous showerhead is perfect to cool me down and get me ready for the evening. My kidney-shaped bathtub faces the floor-to-ceiling window to the ocean, and I hear the jets of the Jacuzzi twirling the water around. My housekeeper must have seen me coming up the walkway and prepared the bath for me. No shower, no quickie here. She knows me so well! I slip out of my summer dress, let it glide to the floor and step into the hot bath. Mmm – the smell of lavender. Disappearing under the small bubbles of water mixed with the fragrant smell of the flowers I realize that I forgot to put my hair up. Too late now! I come up for air, turn off the jets and relax. I must have fallen asleep for a while, because Isabelle, my housekeeper, calmly had put her hand on my shoulder and with a twinkle in her eye, she softly says, "Madame, dinner is almost ready." I just love her French accent! Holding a big, white, soft bath towel in front of her, she is waiting for me to get out of the tub. Reluctantly I stand up and allow her to wrap the towel around me. With another smaller towel she wraps my hair and then hands me the lotion to gush on my skin. I reach for one of my cozy bathrobes and slip into it. Brushing my hair, I ask, "Isabelle, wasn't it the most beautiful day today?"

To which she answers, "Oui, Madame! Every day is the most beautiful day for you."

She is handing me a white silk blouse and a matching long skirt. I slip into them. We both smile at each other, and I am ready to descend to the first floor. I walk by one of the other two bedrooms, those doors are closed. For a split second I am tempted to stop and knock. I lift my hand and – no, I am not going to disturb him. He still must be tired! He flew in from Buenos Aires this afternoon. He deserves some rest. I will greet him at the dinner table. Quietly I turn away from the door and walk toward the staircase. At the top of the stairs I move the lever of the dimmer to the recessed lights, giving the two-story room a feeling of the oncoming night with soft lighting. Walking down the stairs, my hands touch the bronze-colored railing, which reminds me a little bit of Vienna, where I am from. What am I thinking again? It's totally different, not as ornamented as the ones in the castles, very sleek and contemporary. I let out a small laugh and shake my head about myself. I can hear the rings holding the drapes clinking against the pole. The breeze feels great and a whiff of – oh my God – the dessert sneaks into my nostrils. I don't pay attention to anything else and fly into the kitchen, stopping short in front of Michel, my oh-so-French chef, a present from the man upstairs.

"Bon soir Madame, comment vas tu?"

"Tres bien, merci et toi?"

"Toute alleurs, everything is tres, tres bon."

I love to listen to his Franglish. My kitchen suits him well. He is standing at the island in the middle of the room, putting the finishing touches on the tarte aux pommes, his famous apple tart. The taste of the baked apples is lingering in the air and then some other taste is mixed in between, which I discover, is of the main dish. Roasted lamb chops, covered with rosemary, accompanied by sliced new potatoes layered with golden onions and I can see the glass bowl standing next to the sink behind Michel with fresh arugula, endive and radicchio salad. Oh, I can't wait!

"How about some vino?" I ask.

"Vino bianco, or vino rosso?"

"Madame! Monsieur took care of that already."

Oh la-la! I don't have to do a thing tonight! Quelle surprise! So, I sit down on one of the stools, watching Michel placing the lamb chops on the white dinner plates, pouring a tiny dollop of sauce next to it, a little sprig of rosemary, some potatoes and onions and – voila! C'est tout!

My eyes glance over the kitchen. I am glad that I put the rough-looking wooden floor in the kitchen and not the marble. It makes it so much homier this way. The cabinets have a rich brown look – there is one sink on one side of the commercial stove and just to have it my way, I requested a small pizza oven, which my architect placed on the other side of the stove. In case we have a big party and people don't have to step on each other's feet when they are working I have a prep sink in the center island. Behind me is my breakfast nook. Well, it's more like a family room with a window seat, a small table, a desk and a small sofa to lounge around. Off the kitchen is the dining room with windows from floor to ceiling facing the ocean, as are the rest of the rooms in the house. We were even able to get the rooms for my help to have ocean view.

Hmm, why is the door closed? Oh well.

"Voila!" Michel finished mixing the salad and has placed the plates on a tray, so we are ready to go to the dining room. I open the door and gulp; then I let out some sound I never heard myself making before. Lit candles are everywhere. Pink, white and red roses in several vases are around the room, with soft dance music coming from the speakers, which "Monsieur" obviously only put on for the dining room. He is standing there with two champagne flutes in his hands, smiling at me, proud that he was able to pull this off to surprise me.

"Happy day, my love!" he says, grinning from one ear to the other. He opens his arms, walks over to me and kisses me.

I look at him, take one glass and welcome him home. "Thank you so very much. This is quite a surprise!"

"Come with me, I have to show you something."

"The food is getting cold."

"It will only take a minute."

How can I resist his charm? We place our glasses on the credenza at the side of the oblong glass dinner table. My eyes quickly brush over my favorite table setting. Large green grassy-looking leaves as mats, green linen napkins rolled up exquisitely and fanned out while held together by a silver bird napkin ring. Monsieur gently pulls me into the living room and suddenly I realize what happened to me when I came into the house after the beach. Something seemed strange; but the music, the smell of dinner and the desire to quickly be done with my shower took my mind somewhere else rather than paying attention to my surroundings. I am literally floored. Here I am standing in my living room, which was beautiful to begin with. Now it is completely revamped. Two new deep white sofas with enormous cushions grace each side of the fireplace. In between the sofas hovers a large coffee table with inlaid marble right in front of the fireplace. The burning wood is crackling in sync with the music – so it seemed – I feel the hand on my shoulder turning me around and there it is – my dream armoire. I start crying tears of joy. I can't believe my eyes.

Monsieur takes my chin in his hand, turns my face to the other end of the room, points his arm toward a fabulous black, shiny grand piano and softly says, "Happy birthday my love."

"Thank you, thank you, thank you so much." I feel my heart in my throat, my hands are shaking and I sink into his arms to compose myself. My goodness, he must have had ten people here this afternoon doing all that moving around and bringing the new furniture. The room is perfect. Half facing one of the sofas is a chaise, covered in an animal print and next to it is another low square coffee table. I am walking toward it. Actually, it's a chess table with crystal chess figures on top ready to be played and one small 18th century French chair stands beside the table.

"Dinner is served!" Michel's voice brings me back, and we both walk into the dining room. How romantic, with all the candles and the fragrance of the roses; I am ecstatic. The lamb chops are roasted to perfection and melt in my mouth, the potatoes are tender; mixed with the slight tangy taste of the onions; the salad is excellent and crisp and cool. We almost empty the bottle of champagne and start getting very lovey-dovey. I pull myself away from the table, slip into the kitchen and get the Tarte aux Pommes...

Ahh, I can see me and someone in that house for sure. OK, back to reality.

Life is happening. I am learning to exercise more patience, and God willing, everything is slowly and surely falling into place. I am still working four different jobs, and I feel it at the end of the day. If I don't train in the morning, I won't do it at all. So I roll out of bed at 6 am now and do my stuff, 5 am is too early – too much. I realize that I didn't work this hard ever in my life. Sacrifices, sacrifices, no matter what it is in life you want, sacrifices have to be made.

I have the perfect solution: do it when you are young and strong. It's easier then! OK, that didn't work out so well for me, and it definitely was less stressful as long as it lasted when I was 16. Then, it was fun to go to the track and compete against my school mates. I knew that I was doing well, because my times were better. I threw the shot put further, and my long jump was not bad, either. I had no worries in the world then other than about my Dad.

These days I see so many young athletes who have complete support from their parents. What a freeing feeling it must be.

October 12, 2008

Two weeks ago I decided to start working the stairs in Santa Monica twice a week. Monday morning I was there at 8 am, and I walked the steps four times. I was a little out of breath, and my legs were a teensy wobbly, but I made it. Then on Thursday I went again, and it felt better. I thought about doing them one more time, and then I was thinking, *OK, I did exactly what my coach told me to do before the qualification. So I don't have to prove anything right now. And who knows, maybe she has other plans for me.* The following Monday morning, I did the same old four times – there are 189 steps – and then I went home, did my stretching routine, went downstairs into the gym and worked with weights. The next day I felt my chest and my muscles, so now I know I have to concentrate a little more on my upper body.

Tuesday I had a very long conversation with my coach, who advised me about what to do differently on the steps. First time around going up, jog the first partition, then walk the second and alternate to the top. Then the second time around take one step at the time at the first partition, and then the next one take two steps and alternate. The third time do like the first. And the last time one step and two steps. Oh boy, oh boy! That was quite a difference than walking up. I did the entire exercise in 20 minutes – could I do it faster? Not right now, that's for sure! I am happy that I was able to finish and not fall apart. I really was thinking that my legs are getting much stronger.

Today I was jogging three blocks from my real estate office to check out a condo for my client, and I was out of breath. Gee, what the heck is that all about? I couldn't believe it! Now I am thinking, maybe I had to start taking care of my breathing. No, I have to start running again, and I know this will be crucial for getting my physical therapy. OK, I am going to jog in the park tomorrow morning, and then I have a 10 am appointment for a listing presentation, so the steps have to wait until in the afternoon. No way that I am going to skip that, no way!

Tomorrow I am going to make some phone calls, and something great is going to happen. I know it, I feel it, I can smell it. What do I feel all of a sudden again? Fear! That terrible feeling of going out there, being rejected and then not having the opportunity to do something with my life! I am not sure how long this will take until I don't get into that anymore; I only know that I am sick of it, and for some reason I can't shake it.

People see me as successful, tough, strong, powerful and determined and then – here I am – feeling like a little nobody. I don't feel this way all the time; I feel it when I am alone, by myself and imagine nothing is going to happen to change my situation. It's around and around and around like a mouse on a wheel. Well, this is going to change, hopefully soon, I can't stand myself this way. There is no way that I can laugh when I am in that frame of mind, and I can't make other people laugh, either. That makes me more miserable, and then I get stressed out, and then I feel all the different pains in my body, and then I don't want to be with people at all. But there is a good thing; I can't afford to do that, so I decided to make a step in the right direction. Tomorrow I will go to that presentation with the owner of the company, who is a top producer, and I will listen to how she is pitching herself to get a listing. Somehow I have the feeling that the owner of the house is not going to put the house on the market, because right now he is not going to get the price he wants for it. This is great exercise and a fabulous opportunity to watch one of the best realtors. I am a fast learner, so I will get something out of it.

I was praying to my Dad, my Mom and my sister to help me and push that cloud away. I need help to clear my vision and understand what I have to do. I am not afraid of doing as long as I know what it is. So, these are trying times, but I know that I am not alone. Of course it doesn't make it easier at all. I am surrounded by people who are in the same boat. It feels like we are going upstream and have no paddles. Well, I guess that's why I have to strengthen my upper body, so I can make use of my arms and get to the finish line without sinking. Amen!

Yes, of course I could lean on someone's shoulder, but I do not like to do that; not unless it is really necessary, and there is no other way for me to solve an issue by myself. So, I am climbing that mountain by myself, because these are my issues and my issues alone. All these thoughts and more were tumbling through my head like little munchkins, clouding my vision and driving me nuts. When I do have a clear mind, I realize all this is so unimportant in the big scheme of things, and whatever goes through my head is only intensified because I am still wrestling with my father.

October 14, 2008

I wasn't able to go to the stairs yesterday, because I had an early appointment for that listing presentation. The wife of the real estate broker's president and I went to the house. We waited, but nobody was there. Needless to say, I was a little upset to have missed a great opportunity to learn from a pro.

So this morning, I decided to do the stairs. I went a little earlier than normally. That turned out to be great, there were fewer people, and I happily went down the stairs, ready to do my routine. First partition jogging, second partition walking, and third partition jogging...in the middle I felt like being nailed to the ground. I wasn't able to jog to the end of the partition. Next partition I walked up, then I started to jog, couldn't finish it again...On top of the stairs I was out of breath. I drank some water, stretched my legs and went downstairs again. This time it was easier; I took one step and then two steps at the time, a little out of breath but OK. Third time around again, couldn't finish the partition where I was jogging, and I became really irritated. I finished the fourth time, and then it hit me like a ton of bricks.

While walking away from the stairs, I choked and started crying. I couldn't stop. I plunked myself into the seat of my car and cried hysterically, spitting up mucus, coughing, crying, choking and spitting and more. After calming down and with thoughts racing through my brain, I started the car and drove off. On my way home, I thought that maybe the new supplements I am taking are the cause of helping me eliminate all those toxins in my body, and by working my legs so hard, maybe that's it.

It also entered my mind that my legs have felt like lead when I was sprinting at the qualification. I sent an email to my nutritionist asking him about that, and he confirmed that the supplements are there to help eliminate the toxins. Boy, I am full of shit, so to speak. Lovely! Well, I guess it's better now than never and even better than getting me sick.

I realize that I am really very good in suppressing all my issues and pushing them down into the belly of the beast. Now is the time to face my monster again and tame it once and for all, I hope. Today I was a little less positive and uplifting, so I retreated and went home to work from there, so I don't have to explain why I am not making everyone laugh, why I am not my usual perky self. People are so used to seeing me making jokes, laughing, giving everyone a hug and supporting them. When I am in one of those moods, people always ask me what is wrong, and it is difficult for me to show people in business that I, too, have moments of emotional turmoil. It seems to me that those moments are becoming more frequent. They are turning into days and sometimes even weeks.

I called a casting agency this afternoon, and on Thursday I am going to register. Who knows, maybe I can get work in a soap or in a movie or a commercial. I am actually happy right now. I did something to get out of this doldrums situation. Yeah baby, we shall overcome!

Had a lovely phone conversation with Christian, my new friend and he invited me to meet for dinner.

October 15, 2008

Ahhh...yesterday evening! It all started when I stood in front of my closet looking at all my clothes, not sure what I should wear. A dinner date, and I was in a frenzy! I put on a pair of slacks, changed into the only skirt I have, changed again into slacks, then tights with a long sweater, back to slacks. I drove myself nuts until I chose a pair of black slacks, a grey silk blouse and, to top it off, I put my ruby red Pashmina around my shoulders. OK, ready for my date!

My emotional state of mind was somewhere out there; I was not quite sure which way to turn. On one hand, I am really excited to be involved with someone. On the other hand, I am getting a little nervous, because I was not sure how far I wanted to take this and who knows what he is thinking and wanting from me. Dinner last night was scrumptious, conversation was inspiring and the chemistry between us – smoldering! Holding hands, smiles across the table during dinner, hugs and kisses in the car and then – fleeing the scene by using the excuse that I had to get up early in the morning to train. With my heart beating like a sledge hammer against my chest, I raised my hand to wave good-bye through the car window, turned away and then – abruptly turned back, opened the car door and asked, "Would you like to come upstairs?"

He answered, "What about tomorrow?"

I shook my head, got back into the car and showed him to the garage. We slipped through the side door of the building to the security of my apartment without anyone seeing us. I felt like the tenants would scold me, knowing what I was about to do. What followed was like out of a movie. Right behind the apartment door we started kissing like crazy kids, ripped each other's clothes off, fell over Moses, my cat, who definitely was not used to anything like that, and we started laughing. Half-dressed, half-naked, I went into the kitchen, got two glasses and poured champagne. Christian came from behind and peeled me out of whatever else was left on my body, which was not a lot, just my open blouse and my bra. Barely taking a sip of champagne he picked me up, walked over to my sofa and gently placed me there. Moses did not like that and jumped onto the side of the sofa and meowed. I talked to him and then we got up and I dragged Christian into my bedroom and closed the door.

All my worries about not being good enough, all the voices were still when I gave into my desire to be with the man I was so very much attracted to. There were fleeting moments of doubt about what I was doing, and they left as quickly as they appeared. We spent some time lying still and silently gazing into each other's eyes. All of a sudden it was like both of us felt it's time to go. Christian took a brief shower, and after I got him out of the garage I happily went back into bed and snuggled with my cat.

October 16, 2008

This morning I went to the Santa Monica stairs early around 7 am, and I did a lot better than Tuesday. I still huffed and puffed, and my legs were a little wobbly, but I felt much better, and I didn't cry and choke and spit. After the stairs I dragged my butt into the gym for a little weight training and then breakfast.

The rest of the day was filled with work and telephone calls. It went by so fast, that in the evening I felt I had just gotten up.

October 18, 2008

Yesterday evening I was invited to join a group of women to a channeling gathering. We were seven women, including the hostess, the channel. After introducing ourselves, we sat around the table, focusing on our breath and connecting to the earth. I received so much energy that my body was shaking. The last time I had this experience, which actually was my first time, I was in New York with the Korean Masters of the Dahn training. We were in upstate New York in the mountains doing our breathing exercises, and while I was sitting on the ground opening myself to the energy, I received so much that I bounced off the rock I was sitting on. I got so scared and didn't know what I was supposed to do. I felt like being in a different dimension. Two of the Korean Masters came over to hold me until I calmed down.

This time, though, I knew if I opened myself to receive more energy, I would fall off the chair and that was not necessary. I have enough energy right now. I know how to channel it. I was silently asking for guidance and, sure enough, while I was listening to the different questions some of the women asked, I felt something behind me, and then light poured into my chest. I looked and asked its name, and I received something like Avram or Agra.

I googled both names and found out that Agra is a city in India where the Taj Mahal is located, and Avram is the ancient name for Abraham. So, now I am calling on Agra and Avram to support me, help me and guide me. I enjoyed this interesting experience, and on my way home I asked myself what to make of it. This morning I was meditating, and my third eye opened again. All I can see right now is purple and white light. I am not sure how to focus more on the third eye. I always lose connection.

In the afternoon I received a phone call from one of my friends asking me if I could organize a couple's home and office. I immediately felt blessed and accepted the offer. Right away I thanked the Universe for watching out for me and providing me an opportunity to be of assistance, and I honestly experienced lightness and joy. I truly have so much in my life, and I am healthy. So, why am I still beating myself up sometimes? Why is it that there is so much doubt about my ability to take care of myself? Why can't I shake it, shut the voices out and believe in myself?

November 1, 2008

How Love, Fear, Faith and Understanding Work Together. People often ask, "How do I get rid of my fears?" It is either that or something similar to that. Fortunately, the answer is very simple. Once you get into the answer, everything becomes very simple, and fear lets go just like that! Let us have a look now...

We will start by looking at these four things and their opposites. Love comes from within. The opposite of love is no love. Often, people have said that the opposite of love is fear, and in an abstract way that is correct. It is correct because, generally, you tend to have either one or the other. When fear is absent, you feel the love that is always there. When fear comes in, you are blinded from the love. But, upon closer observation, you will notice that you can have both emotions running over the same thing. So in a direct sense, the opposite of love is no love. Love is acceptance; so the opposite of love can also be called non-acceptance.

Fear, as we have seen, is a separate emotion. Fear is false evidence appearing real. You fear because you doubt your capability to handle something or create a successful outcome. Otherwise you would not fear if you did not doubt your ability not to be touched by that which you fear. In truth, there is nothing to fear. It may not be evident now why this is so, or it may be. Either way, you will see it soon. There is nothing to fear. Anyway, fear is what blocks your feeling of love within, and with that it takes your power away simply because power is vested in love. Force is vested in fear and sometimes force looks like power, but it isn't even close in comparison and lasting effect. So now we know that fear is what obscures love and power. The question then remains, what gets rid of fear or what allows fear?

Well, what is the opposite of fear? It is no fear. No fear is the opposite of fear. How do you get to no fear?

Fear comes in when faith is not there. Faith is more than believing. Faith is closer to knowing than to believing.

When you know, you know. It's like when you go to pick up a glass of water and drink it, you don't doubt you will manage. You just drink knowing it works. That is knowing. A slight step behind knowing is faith. When you have faith, you pretty much know you are fine, one way or another, despite appearances to the contrary. When you have no faith, you get fear. And that is the key to removing fear, having faith. So how do you have faith?

With understanding. Understanding ensures faith, simply because you know how things work. Think of a time you felt confused and incapable because you missed the information, and then when you got the information and understanding, you had peace and you knew you could easily do what you had previously feared.

Understanding of how life works, how life works, is the key. Take a look under the hood of life, into the machinery behind life, and with that new immense understanding you will have automatic faith. It is a loop. You have faith because you know how it works, and so you have faith that it works.

And as a bonus to understanding, you have peace within yourself and with others.

And so the first step to all these things, to having faith, eliminating doubt and fear, to having peace, is all in getting an understanding. Not just any understanding. Things are in layers. There is a layer that is the foundation, a causative layer, and a layer that is the superficial, the effect layer that is built on the foundation.

The understanding of the causal layer is one we are talking about here. Fortunately, there is much available to us nowadays in terms of high-level wisdom and insights.

Seek them and understand, if you wish to have the key out of the box. You may also have a look at the book What If You Knew The Answer To and the Reason For Everything In Your Life, *which is available at www.imagesofone.com and looks into the completeness of the understanding we are talking about here.*

I wish you success and wellbeing.
Article written by David Cameron, CEO
ImagesOfOne.com.

I was reading this today in one of my emails, and it was a perfect explanation for how I feel. It says it all! When I read something other people write, I very easily understand and comprehend what I have to do and how I have to think; and then, when I am by myself and alone for a while the fear comes back and I forget to shut it down. I am going to do that consciously from now on. I will have that power to eliminate fear from my life. I do!

Training has been good lately; my stretching exercises are getting easier. Yes, I still feel my muscles when I stretch a little longer and more extensively, but it is not as painful as it was months ago.

I am playing with the thought of following up with that casting agency, the one that I didn't go to a couple of weeks ago. Why not? Darn, I got too busy with something, and then I thought, maybe they tell me I am too this or too that. I really feel silly to have these thoughts of self-doubt. So, we'll see what happens. I miss the action around the theater and movie sets. I am always busy in the office and the building. Waiting and thinking that some casting director is going to have this brilliant idea to call me is really ridiculous, because nobody in the entertainment industry knows of me.

I was thinking of my "Monster." What is my Monster? The other day when I was exercising, my financial situation ripped through my mind, and I was angry that the fear of not having enough money didn't lose its grip even during my training. I was thinking of my book, *What's Your Monster's Name?* and also about the training. Suddenly I realized that it was not the running, or better, the lack of it, for so many years. Was it my writing? Or the fear of it?

I am still apprehensive at times to write, and it hit me. When my father broke the lock to my diary and ripped open the pages to see what I had written, my heart sank. I felt so violated; at that moment I wanted to sink into the earth, disappear, vanish into another world. I was so young, and there was nothing he wouldn't do to hurt me, nothing to make me feel lower than dirt. And, of course, I stopped writing at that point.

When I am thinking of that time, I vaguely remember that those two incidents may have been close together; but then it really doesn't matter; maybe the diary incident came before and that got me into running – running away from this monster, who I thought, was my father.

I understand now that seeking professional help to get over the abuse would have given me a better insight at an earlier stage in my life. The experience with a psychiatrist in Vienna shortly after my father's death, who screamed at me, prevented me from trusting any doctor.

November 16, 2008

Wow! Sixteen days went by, and I haven't written one word into my journal. I have been busy with a lot of things, but not with myself; my inner world!

I finally made my way to the casting agency to find out if they would take me for background work in TV and film. I went out to Burbank on October 23rd and signed up. I was all excited! Then on October 24, I received this email

FEMALE, AGE 50+ MODELS WANTED
TO PARTICIPATE IN AN EPIONE
DOCUMENTARY FILM PROGRAM

I sent them a short bio with two pictures, and two days later they called me for a short interview. I was confident that I was going to get the part, and the day after the interview they called me and told me, "You are the girl!" I was ecstatic! Here I signed up for work and then I got the chance to get a little makeover, make me look fresher – great! Filming was scheduled for that Friday; it was postponed until the following Monday, which prolonged the waiting period. Having the healing period postponed and not being able to take advantage of the weekend made me a little antsy, but there was nothing I could do.

Over the weekend I had to prepare my skin with some cream. That was uncomfortable, and I looked like a tomato. Not being used to my skin looking like that at all, I freaked.

Thank goodness the weekend went by fast. Monday morning at the doctor's office preparation for the laser treatment began with more creams, then washing everything off and then numbing cream and then we started with camera work. I was being interviewed and asked why I chose this method over surgery. "I am not keen of having my face all cut up and in the end look like every other woman who had plastic surgery; that is the reason".

Pretty quickly the doctor was ready for me and then – what can I say – it began, and within a few minutes it all was over. I felt some cold air blowing onto my face, and I heard the buzzing sound of the laser and that was it.

After it was all over, I received instructions on what I had to do over the next few days, and I waited for my friend to pick me up and drive me home.

Icepacks, icepacks and more icepacks and lots of rest for the next few days! I dared to look into the mirror and saw Frankenstein's daughter. I had to laugh; here I thought I would look gorgeous, no wrinkles, no lines, and what I saw was a bruised face. Of course, I never had the experience of doing anything major to my face, so after a few days I started to heal, and Ingrid came back out. I am still peeling a little around my cheeks. I started to venture out and see people who know me, and they were all telling me that my face looked great.

Of course I am being extremely critical with myself, so I am still seeing a little swelling under my eyes. I know this, too, shall pass, and in about one week we are going to film the result. What an experience!

While I was holed up at home – not to scare away people – I worked on the instruction book for my previous martial arts school to help getting it done. I also started sending out farming letters for my real estate business.

My training was put on hold for two weeks, and tomorrow it's back to getting into shape again. I have been extremely careful with my diet during the past two weeks, because I was not able to do any training or even work out. It will be interesting, to say the least, feeling my muscles again. I can't wait!

December 22, 2008

Two days before Christmas and thoughts of how I celebrated Christmas in New York with my former husband and my stepchildren made me smile. That was quite a production! Every year we had a 14-foot tree with thousands of little lights strung around the branches and hundreds and hundreds of beautiful original handmade ornaments. I worked on putting up the tree for days. I love Christmas! What can I say? I am still like a little girl waiting for Santa Claus to put the presents under the tree. No 14-foot tree now! My cat I had at that time, Mischa, loved to climb the tree and have a "fiesta" playing with all the ornaments. All of my ornaments ended up with an organization, because after the divorce I moved to a tiny little apartment, and I had no room for anything. Little did I know how precious those were when I first went out to buy a few ornaments. Things change, and now I decorate the house, so my kitty Moses doesn't get tangled up in anything. It will be quiet on Christmas Eve, and that's all right with me.

I am still training every day. I don't have the enthusiasm right now. Holiday blues, I guess, have taken over and occupy my mind more than stretching my muscles, which tell me every morning be careful, don't push, you may hurt yourself. Christian has left for Chicago, and I won't see him for a while. Of course the thought came up, if I will see him at all. There it is again; that little monster called fear of not being worthy.

December 26, 2008

Oh, what fun it is to ride in a one-horse open sleigh. Not in Southern California. Watching Christmas movies and getting into the spirit kept me sane. I even went to a couple of dinners at friends' homes. It was so nice to be with families and children and experience the joy of Christmas.

I am grateful for having the opportunity to be around people at this time of the year. Thank you.

December 31, 2008

Barely making out the contours of the plant in the living room I walk upstairs to take advantage of the morning's stillness, which is hovering in the room. It is right before dawn, and the night is slightly giving way to this last day of 2008.

You seem to be here with me. Your energy is circling through the air, and when I close my eyes I can see your face in front of me.

I bow my head and let you touch my hair. Tears of gratitude flow from my eyes down to my chin, landing on my shirt. I miss you so!

My decision to end this year on a high note is giving me the freedom to be romantic and at peace, even though I am by myself and will celebrate New Year's Eve alone.

Preparation for the National Games

January 1, 2009

My New Years' resolution: I will conquer my fears; I will persevere. And I am training and getting stronger and faster. And I am winning a medal in August of 2009. I am doing what I love to do. I am writing and publishing my books. And I am traveling, taking a vacation. And I am inspiring people to live their dream – and this is it! Merry, happy and a fabulous New Year to me and everyone in the world!

January 22, 2009

Today, after my physical therapy, I went to the office for a little while, and then I got into my car to drive home. At the first intersection I had to stop for the light to change. Scanning the sidewalk, my eyes were pulled toward this man at the garbage bin. He was leaning over; at the next moment he was sliding onto the ground and dropped down next to the bin.

Suddenly it hit me: he was on drugs! Within a blink of an eye I was remembering the time when I took cocaine, and how I could have been that person; I could be dead now. I took a deep breath. Tears filled my eyes, and I said out loud, "Thank you, God, for saving my life. Thank you, God, for saving my life." The light changed, and I drove off.

How can I describe the feeling; the feeling of gratitude that I am alive and well and healthy? How far have I come to find myself, to get in touch with my feelings and not feel fear of being ridiculed or punished? I realize how blessed I am that I was able to stop using cocaine from one minute to the next and never touched it again, ever!

Growing up in Vienna, I never used drugs, I didn't even know about them, other than hearing that in Amsterdam people used to smoke hashish. That was the extent of my knowledge. When I met my American husband, he told me about grass, and I seriously asked him if people really smoke grass, the one that grows on the ground. I was so naïve! When I moved to the States, I smoked with him. What went through my head was this: I didn't want to be like my mother, not drinking nor smoking cigarettes. My father found that boring, so he ended up with a mistress. Those were my thoughts and rationalization. I was not going to end up like my mother; I was going to do everything my husband asked me to do, and I did. Smoking pot escalated to using cocaine. He convinced me that I couldn't get addicted to it and his words, "Don't worry, everybody does it and I am here to protect you." made me feel secure.

Well, after some years of using, he must have gotten tired of me and found someone else. I always had enough supply, and cocaine high made me feel I was accomplishing something important, even though I was doing nothing more than cooking, cleaning, washing clothes, going shopping, making dinner, taking care of the children and turning into a skinny, bitchy person. So in a way, I did end up like my mother – not the bitchy part. The only difference was that my father died at a very young age, and my husband divorced me. I was completely devastated. I never believed that he would go that far. I thought that he wanted to teach me a lesson, threatening me with a divorce, so I'd sober up, and see what's happening to me and us. I stopped using years before the divorce, so I felt like I was the good wife then, and how could he leave me? He did! After the initial shock and lots of tears and blaming myself, I attended seminars and more seminars and workshops and talked to a lot of people to find answers. Little by little – literally – I uncovered the person I thought I was supposed to be. Still no "professional" help.

Nineteen years have passed since my divorce, and I believe that I finally feel completely comfortable with who I am. There are moments – no, sometimes days – when the old thought patterns and fears are creeping up or maybe the old way of reacting to something someone says. Now I am able to recognize them and put them away, realizing how I have grown. I am proud of my accomplishments, and I love myself for doing all that hard work. It pays off! One step at a time.

Right now, I can work on just being and going back to training – ***yeah***!

February 3, 2009

Yesterday I went to Manhattan Beach and was jogging without pain. Then I walked up the sand dune twice. I was surprised about how much easier it seemed than last year. This gives me hope that I can truly do something about my speed. I have six months until the Senior Olympics. I made a contract with myself that I am eliminating alcohol; no more sip of red wine or a margarita with my friend at happy hour. No more caffeine, which includes chocolate and sugar and sweets and strudels and cakes and cookies, and, and...That reminds me:

when was I last at Happy Hour? I guess I won't miss the margarita.

What will be the most difficult; sugar! I also read a long article about alkaline and acidity, and it freaked me out. I know that my body is a little on the acidic side. Now I want to be really careful to be eating food supplying more alkaline for my body. It will be a little challenging; so what! I have been going through challenges almost all my life and dealt with them. Now I am a little more aware of them and more used and set in my ways. I want to accomplish something, and that something takes more than a walk in the park. We'll get there; my body and I.

I also started to meditate more to balance myself and get grounded and clear about what I am going to do in the near future, rather than doing the same old thing every single day and not accomplish anything. My phone calls, my emails to clients, my visits to clients don't seem to get me anywhere right now. For some reason, I get the feeling that I am supposed to do something different, and real estate was another stepping stone in my life and then maybe not. Ha – here is that thought again! Silly me.

Tonight I will go to bed with the thought to get clarity about my future. Maybe I will have one of my dreams. I am curious about what I will see. Good night!

February 23, 2009

It has been a challenging 20 days since my last entry. The long drawn-out battle about receiving my commission for the commercial lease has had its grip on me. For some reason I was not able to get through to the listing agent. He refused to communicate with me and only this morning I asked myself why I am allowing these things to happen. How can I not have had clear sailing during this last transaction?

Friday evening when I went to a spiritual gathering and spoke to the teacher, that knot in my head untied. What came out was that I didn't own the situation. I gave away my power to my client, who in his caring way didn't know that his request to handle the agent would drag this issue out and I, showing respect, allowed it to happen. I should have taken control and explained to my client that I appreciate his assistance and still, I do have to take care of MY business.

What a lesson I have learned! That will never happen to me again. Or better, I will not allow it to happen. Focusing on my goal to publish my other book, *What's Your Monster's Name?*, is moving ahead. There is still fear of not being able to do it on my own, and, and, and…I just have to do it - fearfully!

Training has been OK; I am still training without my coach being present at the work out. She has been in contact with me and sent a list of what I have to do each week. I am now visualizing how I am going to win, and that was a challenge, because I visualized myself at the qualification sprint where I came in third, and that doesn't help. So, I have to go back to the time when I was 16 and I ran the last leg of the 100 meter hurdle relay and we won. And to top it off, we set a new record for that state in Austria.

My physical therapist told me that I need orthotics, so next week I should get them. I will have to wear them in all my shoes, not just my running shoes. That will be fun! Whatever it takes. I am going to get help to be in tip-top shape in August. If that doesn't help to get rid of that uncomfortable feeling in my hip flexor muscles, then we have to do something else to heal that, because I want to excel and get faster to win this race! Boy, I already won the race! I am competing; I overcame one of the "Monsters" in my head. Now I would love to win a medal at the Nationals.

Focus, focus, focus – I really need to keep my focus on what is coming next, and that's the race in August. Publishing the other book has been on my mind, too. Keeping my eyes on my goals in itself is distracting, because there are more than one goals. I am in the process of getting my clients to make an offer on a house they have been viewing a couple of times. They are having a big challenge making a decision. I believe it is going to happen soon, or something else has to come their way they fall in love with. I am going to have some headshots taken and register with another casting agency, maybe that will give me a different perspective. I do have fun working in film and TV. That shouldn't be that difficult, right?

Working around artistic people always gives me a high. I miss the excitement of the theater, the fast pace of the time when I was modeling in Europe, which seemed like a different lifetime ago.

Reading through my last entry made me realize how many times I used the word focus. It frazzles me that I am all over the place. It also makes me smile. There are so many things in my head that I would like to accomplish, that I probably would be bored if only focusing on one thing. Running will be priority right now.

March 1, 2009

I attended my first Toastmaster session yesterday. This is very interesting and exiting! I already prepared my speech, which will probably not happen for another three weeks, because one has to be a member. Next week I am joining a networking group with women entrepreneurs. That should be a great experience.

Right now I can't wait to make things happen and start a new chapter in my life. How many times have I said that already? On the other hand, a book has many chapters. And when I think about it, life is a book. So why am I so opposed to having different chapters? Isn't it much better to look forward to a better chapter instead of lingering in the old and depressing one? YEAH, you bet it is! I am getting the hang of it. Not that I am moody or depressed when I am with people. I do have a positive attitude and make people smile; it's when I am at home by myself that I am thinking and thinking and thinking and nothing positive seems to come out. In essence, I am stuck in a chapter, and it seems funny when I think about it. I am so aware of it, too, and still...

Boy, oh boy, oh boy, I realize what I am doing to myself! I have been beating myself up again. Nobody else does it. And if someone is making an attempt, I am stopping them in their tracks. And no more socializing with them, period.

There is this mantra in my head my father drilled into me. Do the best you can, always. What does it mean to be second best? Nothing. I get up in the morning, I train, I go to work and I am nice to people. I would love to have a little more fun. My attempt to accomplish that has been minimal. Tomorrow morning is gym training and then on Monday steps in Santa Monica. I am shooting for the sand dunes in Manhattan Beach on Thursday. Maybe track after that. My physical therapist said to me that I have to break in my orthotics first by walking in them and after a week or so then maybe I can start running in them. I am wearing them inside my running shoes when I am at home now. They only come off when I go to bed. Doing all this, which is necessary to get rid of the uncomfortable feeling in my hip flexor, is not very painful. It just bothers me, and it is restrictive to my movements.

Tomorrow I am going to show some homes to one of my clients, and I feel that things are moving for me. Well, it is up to me to make things move. I understand that nothing is going to happen if I sit on the couch and wait for things to come to me. So, tomorrow I am going to finish my taxes. That has been hanging over my head, and I have been procrastinating to do them for an entire month. Boy, that does not make me feel good about myself! I, Ingrid, am procrastinating. Wow, I admitted it. So, now I can take charge and change that. OK, I will...good night - until tomorrow morning; it is actually today already...time to go to bed.

April 27, 2009

What a month and a half! Business has been picking up, and one of my clients made an offer on a condo, which was accepted, so now we are in escrow. I am also working with a few other people who are anxious to buy a home. God willing everything is going to work out for everyone. I am looking forward to more excitement

My 66th birthday came and went. My dearest friend came over and showered me with the most wonderful orchids I have ever seen, and I received a very generous gift. All my friends have been extremely supportive and helped in every which way I can imagine. I am truly blessed and very grateful for the love and affection I am receiving.

Besides that I have been training more than only running. My plan was to fly to New York, where my acupuncturist guru lives. He healed me from having awful migraine headaches, and I haven't had a headache in 19 years. I need him to take care of my IT band and my hip flexor muscles, so I will be able to run in August without pain and win! The trip was postponed because of business. I have to be careful with the way I train, stretch and sprint until I am able to get to New York – hopefully in one month.

My life has become more isolated during the last year, and that's not who I am. I am a happy person, who wants to laugh and have fun and also be entertaining to the people around me. I was wondering about my life in general and how it happened to become so monotone and not exciting at all. The last few days I had fun with my clients and was making jokes with my colleagues, and I felt alive again for the first time in a long time. Nothing drastic has happened, and not a lot has changed; I haven't won the lottery – yet, because one has to buy a ticket to win…LOL. And I have to acknowledge that it is mind over matter. It is all in my head, and taking the liberty to make that decision that it can't go on like that anymore and change my attitude makes a world of difference in my behavior toward people.

I can smile again from the inside out, and I believe people recognize that. It makes me feel different than being nice and calm and composed and – boring! I am alive again. I can't wait to do something outrageous again, maybe win the 100 meters at the Senior Games in August! An idea popped into my head and made me aware of the difference between my life in Austria and then in New York and now. In Austria I was a young model and actress, and work was never an issue. I wanted to work, I called my agent, and I got booked and I had fun. All the time. In New York I was married, and I was told not to work. No work, no worries. I had someone to take care of me, and we had fun. A lot. Now I have to work, I have to take care of myself, money became important. I had to adapt to the fact that I didn't know anything about business at all. Modeling? Too old. Acting? Too much of an accent. I had to learn a trade, so I went to school and got my real estate license. I was not used to asking for business, it came to me when I lived in Austria and - I was so much younger then. Now I have to compete for it.

May 16, 2009

Started training intensively now that I only have 2-1/2 months left until the Games. In a way, I already want to get it over with. I have been waiting for so long that it almost becomes an anticlimax. Of course, I am also doing this on my own – completely and totally! No coach, no trainer, no sponsors, so I am dealing with work and training and the voices in my head, that I am not going to make it. I am making it, damn you, stop talking to me in that negative way, I hate that. I can't stand it anymore! Why shouldn't I make it? I am going to run and that's that!

Of course, my little ego wants to win, and that's what is happening and making me nuts. My ego! You are not going to win, you are not going to win, you don't have enough training, you really don't know what to do, you are afraid, you don't think you are good enough to deserve to win…and on and on and on it goes. I want to shut that voice up, once and for all! As my martial arts teacher always says, "Your ego is not your amigo."

And then I believe that I am going to have a chance to win; that voice is extremely small and low and tiny, but it is there, and I have to listen to it carefully and nurse it to get bigger and louder.

I am jogging now and sprinting for only a short distance. I am still extremely cautious that I am not going to hurt myself. I went back to Santa Monica and am doing the steps now twice a week. Next week I am going to start with doing them three times, and maybe I will do them six times up and down instead of only four times. That should make my legs a little stronger.

My thoughts have been consumed with training, and I am getting to be in a better place. I know in my heart that I will have to commit to doing what I am supposed to do, which is inspire other people to live their dreams, and then it will all fall into place. As long as I go to work and take care of other people's needs and not mine, I will exist and not live to my full potential. Somehow I know that. I am wondering if anybody else has those same feelings.

My mind wanders to the new relationship. As limited as it seems, it is a distration from everything else I do day in day out. My friend is spending quite some time in Chicago, which makes our dates seem new all the time. It gives me enough freedom to take care of myself and my needs. Having a relationship with someone by my side who enjoys my company and who accepts the limitations without making a commitment to a more serious outcome right now, gives me a feeling of being in control of my own decisions. This time is really about me growing and taking care of my responsibilities and accepting the outcome. No blame, no shame. Looking at myself and loving myself.

May 17, 2009

I am done with my stretching routine, getting ready to go downstairs to the gym. I made my protein smoothie, and for some reason my chest is hurting. It feels like a giant hand is pushing on my chest and my throat. I am yawning, trying to get air out of my body while I am writing. My jaws are bothering me, too. In between writing and yawning, I am pressing my hands below my ribcage to get rid of the pain. My ears hurt, and I have no clue what is happening. I am going to lay down for a while before I am going to go anywhere.

One hour later. I spent some time on my daybed on the patio and concentrated on breathing and must have fallen asleep, because when I woke up, the pain was gone. I am a little confused, but I will go downstairs and work out on the bike.

This afternoon after working out in the gym and getting ready to leave the house, I went to the office before I looked at some open houses in the Valley. I spoke to an old friend, whom I haven't seen in over a year and then drove home. Had a healthy dinner…oops, OMG we are having an earthquake.

Wow, had to look for my cat, who was hiding under the bed. I turned on the TV to check, and we had a 5.0 earthquake. Interesting, the last couple of earthquakes were not sliders. Everything was shaking for a few seconds, and then it was over.

I am thinking, what does that have to do with my training? Maybe everything. My life does not only consist of training, eating, massages, training, eating and sleeping. The earthquake made me aware that something can happen, and in a split second it may be all over. Live, love and laugh a lot.

Again I was told that ionized water is good for the body. I have to look into it and find the appropriate system. ALKALINE! Balance, balance, balance! I will go to sleep now.

My thoughts are all over the place, and I want to focus on winning in every which way. Here is that ominous word again - focus.

Body, Mind and Soul

May 20, 2009

Watching "Brave New Voices" on HBO, with young poets from all over the country. It made me I realize what I had to do. I awoke, literally. Holding the anger and the hatred toward my father in my body for so long made me unaware of its presence – or did it?

I made peace with him on a psychological and mental level, but not on a physical level. All the pain he administered to my body, all the severity of it, is still anchored deep within the tissue of my body. The decision to get rid of it will not be an easy task. I will have to go all the way back and connect with what happened and get it out.

Letter to my father:

Papa,

Look at me! Look at me! Please look at me! Are you happy with what you accomplished? Are you happy having fractured and bruised another human being? Splinters of firewood are embedded in my knees; I remember the hollow sound of my skull hitting the corner of a piece of furniture!

Ping! My ear went ping - and then a scream exited my mouth and pierced the air while soap flowed down my face. I watched in disbelief as a hand flailed toward my face again.

A giant creature lifted this tiny body from the ground, smacking its behind and throwing it to the floor. I lived with a man from hell. Fear crawled up my spine like a snake ready to put its fangs into my neck. The crashing sound of the hand slapping my face made my head turn and my body spin, and I found myself lying twisted on the floor.

Oh, how I dreaded sitting at the dinner table when you were at home with us. You always found a reason to punch your fist into my back, threatening to break it if I didn't sit up straight. Kicking me when I lay curled up on the floor so you don't hit my face. I feared people would ask me what happened, so you kicked my back again and again.

Why did my sister and I have to spend Sunday mornings with you in bed – naked? Why? Why were you angry as you ordered me back into the bed after your erect penis brushed against my body and I jumped away in fear?

I am tired of my self-imposed prison, feeling like I am worth nothing, getting back to beating myself up, again and again and again. Why? Was it not enough that I was beaten by you over and over and over until you exhausted your energy and gave up; until the next day when you found another excuse to trample on me?

I'll tell you what anger can do to a human being. There was a time when I wanted to kill you, I wanted you dead. I was imagining how you'd die in agony while watching the movie of your treacherous accomplishment bringing up Ingrid. You were a godless human being, how could you? What on earth did I do to you? You had the audacity to barge into my life and beat me up because I was afraid and didn't come to you; and then you used me as your punching bag. How was that possible?

Was it my innocence that scared you? Was it the war that screwed you up and made you that hellish thing called a human being? What went through your head each and every time when you raised your hand and beat me? How did it make you feel as you pulled me by my hair and threw me down the stairs? What did you think when you heard me scream when my ear drum burst from you smacking me? What, what, what? Did it remind you of something you wanted to forget? Did you want to kill me? What? Why? Who was I to you? I certainly wasn't a little girl you loved. Crap, I was only three years old when you first laid eyes on me and you took my little body and beat it. What the hell was wrong with you?

You smacked me when I told you that your friend, the professor, touched my breasts, telling me I was stupid for playing with boys when grown men had an interest in me. I was only 7 then! What was that all about? You had me checked by your friend, the gynecologist, at the age of 16 to have me checked to see if I was still a virgin, and he hit on me. You sent me to a psychiatrist to find out what was wrong with me, because I defied you. Why did this man make me run naked up the stairs? For crying out loud, who was that nut? I was surrounded by grown men who used me as what?

I was so angry at you for so many different reasons that I don't even know what to say any more. I want to be done with that chapter of my life. I don't want to cry anymore; you are not worth it. You called me worthless. Well, I'll tell you something. I think you were talking to yourself. I am done with you. I want to be done with you. I let go of you, and I let you rest in peace.

I am shaking right now like all of this happened yesterday. Yet there is a sort of quiet calm within me, knowing that kind of evil feeling has left me and that heavy cloud hovering over my life has lifted, evaporated into nothingness. I can hear the wind whisking away the remnants of some dark memories. They are gone now, they are gone. It is quiet now. Good bye! It makes me so sad that I harbored so many unresolved feelings inside of me. You never allowed me to say one word against you, or to confront you and question your actions, so I swallowed the anger and the hate. It is gone, and you are not here to stop me from spewing it all out and finally getting rid of it. You have no more power over me. I am Ingrid now, the person you never met.

It also saddens me that something made you the way you were, and you missed out on so much in your life. You could have experienced love, joy and happiness with your children and shared with them.

I never knew what a loving father is; I only can imagine and dream and never live it.

Tears are streaming down my cheeks, collecting in a crumpled tissue on my keyboard. Sadness is filling my heart, and I feel so much lighter now. For some reason it seems like my father was waiting for me to speak up.

May 21, 2009

I took a martial arts class this morning with Master Winkle from Virginia. He is also one of my clients. He was recommended by my Master from New York, and I helped him find the property that is now his school.

It was interesting to be in the Dojang on the mat again. We listened to a lot of information about how to apply the philosophy of martial arts to our daily lives, and it was great to be reminded of what I learned so long ago. I did a few kicks and, of course, my IT band acted up again. It seems to me that the culprit of this pain is my knee, so I can't wait to get some acupuncture. I know, I know, I have been saying this for quite a while, and something always comes up and postpones the visit to the acupuncturist. Business comes first, and I have to take care of that.

Anyway, I had a great time doing something even more physical than I normally do. Now it's back to jogging in the park and doing my one, two, three's and sprinting.

May 26, 2009

My friend at the Aurashop gifted me a session with this fabulous woman who is an angel therapist and quantum biofeedback specialist. Her sessions are uniquely designed to balance my energy field, which enhances my physical well-being. She will help me to move beyond personal limitations and discover my infinite possibilities. Each energy session combines the technology of the Quantum SCIO, or "Maggie" pulsed cellular energizer and the soothing color therapy of the Original Light Table. I left this extraordinary session with greater personal insight and a feeling of empowerment to create abundance, love, joy, confidence and more.

Wow, for an entire hour I felt elevated, went deep into Theta state and came back with a renewed awareness of who I really am. Thank you!

May 30, 2009

Oh boy – I did a four-day major body cleansing. I have never done that before in my life. Four days of eating nothing but two spoons of fiber in water five times a day. I was hungry! I was training on top of it, and by the third day I wasn't able to run or lift weights or bike or do anything physical. Not so smart on my part. I had to stop! Today, two days after I was finished, I went back to jog and stretch and eat again. My mind is clear. I am happy. I am making one of my dreams a reality. I am going to participate in the Senior Olympics. Last night I attended a friend's birthday party. I told someone about my dream, and they asked me if I am running every day, which I don't. I realized my dream was not about running; my dream was to be in the Olympics, and that's exactly what this is all about.

I am going to be a part of the Games, no matter how it will end. I am going to live that dream and then go on to my next one. Now I understand what is involved to live a dream or to reach a goal. One has to make that journey to get there. Until now, I was focused on reaching that goal. Psychologically, I was still anchored in the past, feeling that I would not be able to win. That all changed over the past week. Now I am going to do the best I can and know that I will win. I will, I can, I am able. I will run like the wind, effortlessly and with ease. The wings of my angels will help me to fly down that track. Oh, how glorious! Sweet smell of victory! Even if I don't win a medal, I am still winning.

May 31, 2009

What a weekend! Friday night I went to a birthday party, Saturday I attended a bridal shower and a screening of one of the newest movies. I didn't have that much of a social life in a year like this weekend. I guess it's the new Ingrid, back to life! Today I stayed home, taking care of housework that had been staring me in my face for quite a while. I don't like to iron clothes, but it had to be done. Now I can relax for the rest of the day and prepare myself for a week of intense training. I am looking forward to pushing myself a little bit more than before. Yes, I will be careful not to hurt myself, I promise! My goal is to do the Santa Monica steps three times this week, and maybe I can make the dunes in Manhattan Beach. That will make me happy. OK, let's do it! Will let you know how I succeeded.

June 5, 2009

My attempt to eat raw food was cut short. I am allergic to something in the mixture I bought, and my face blew up like a balloon. I looked like Mike Tyson punched my face. My face is itching and red like a tomato. This is now the fourth day after I stopped, and I am still itching. The swelling went down, and I look a little more like me again. I guess my body is telling me to stick with what I am eating and stop trying something radically new.

My fabulously great plans for last week were just that, plans to do the steps and the dunes, and what did I do? Work. Work like there is no tomorrow, so I ended up only training at home, doing my routine. Thursday I took another martial arts class in Burbank after working out at home.

Then came another low blow – at least in my head. I sent an application for a documentary on the Senior Games for PBS and was so psyched. I thought for sure that they would choose me, among others. This afternoon I received an email that they didn't choose me. I was so bummed! So, of course, the voices came up again. *You see, you are not wanted. They don't need you. You are not good enough, you are nothing. What are you trying to prove? Stop it, you are not worth anything.* OMG, my ego and the voices - they don't stop! They are always coming back, and I would like to quiet them and be strong to shut them up. Otherwise I feel sorry for myself and don't do anything. Tomorrow I am going to run and do whatever else I can do. No matter what, I am going to run!

June 19, 2009

Time flew by the last few weeks, and I believe I accomplished a lot. I have been very busy with one of my clients, searching for a new home, and there is a possibility that we found something appropriate for her. It will be a long process, due to the fact that this is a short sale, and we first have to get the acceptance. We shall see.

I received an extremely gracious acknowledgement from World Martial Arts in Burbank for finding the perfect space for them to open their new school in southern California. I call it the Oscar for Realtors. I was truly honored!

Now I've started jogging in the park and also sprinting a little. Carefully though, because my groin and hamstrings are still noticeable, which means I have to be nice to myself. I am learning! Yesterday I finally went to the Santa Monica stairs again. I planned on doing them for such a long time, but every day something came up, and I wasn't able to do them. The Santa Monica Fire department had their guys out there walking, jogging and running up those stairs. I asked their coach how many times they are doing them. He told me that right now they have done them 11 times. I almost fainted.

Nevertheless that inspired me to do them five times, which was a first for me, because normally I do the stairs four times. In between, I even got a little jog in. I felt really good. Never mind that I feel my legs today; it's a good feeling though, and I know this is because I did more than usual. And of course, I haven't been doing the stairs for quite a while. I realize that I need some kind of inspiration to push myself.

Here is that phrase again: push myself. I know from my previous training in HapKiDo when I pushed myself to the point where I hurt myself, and then I wasn't able to train anymore. I literally jeopardized my training to have an excuse for not continuing, because in the back of my mind I still had that gnawing feeling and I heard that oh-so-familiar voice telling me "No!" Now I am pushing to get better and stronger and faster, not weaker to sit on the sidelines and watch other people participating.

I feel really great, and I am getting excited to be even better than I am now. I know I can do it! I will do it! I am able to do it! Yes! One more month and a few days and then it is off to Palo Alto.

June 23, 2009

It took me 23 minutes to get out of bed this morning. By 7 am I was in the car, ready to attack the Santa Monica stairs. At 7:20 am I parked the car, today a little further away from 4th Street. For some reason, parking was sparse. Oh well, so I walked a little more than usual. I prepared my iPod, and in my mind I knew I would do the stairs six times. Coming up the first time walking, jogging, walking, jogging was not so bad at all. I took a sip of water and went back down. Second round! This time was one step, two steps, and I remembered that two weeks ago I couldn't even make it all the way up doing the routine. This time, no problem! I decided to jog around the bend instead of walking down the steps. I did my third time, my fourth time and then I went another one and another one. All in all, I did the stairs eight times. I was playing with the thought to continue and decided against it. I didn't want to push myself too hard and then be on my back for the next few days. I am so happy I accomplished that, and now I am going to do my stretching routine. I also sent an email to my coach, who has been living in another state for quite some time and told her about my current routine. She promised to help me with my speed. Yeah! Hurrah! That's all I need right now. I have to concentrate on getting faster. I realize how much stronger I am this year than last, and I didn't even do that much during the entire past 12 months after the qualification. That makes me wonder how much more could I do, how much stronger would I be, how much faster could I run? Oh well, this is a mute point for right now, because I am as strong as I am, and I run as fast as I run, and only the future will tell. I am happy, though, for right now. And yes, I have to be really aware not to push myself too hard. I have to tell myself that all the time. I need to be gentle with myself.

Tomorrow is another day, and I shall continue.

June 25, 2009

Michael Jackson died today. His body, the visual being, has perished. He is gone. His soul, his music, his message to the world will live on forever. What gift he has given us! Thank you, Michael, may you RIP.

June 28, 2009

What a week it was! Friday I attacked the stairs and managed to do them 12 times! Wow! It all began not even two weeks ago when I watched the firemen going up and down and up and down. What an inspiration they were to me, and that pushed me to do them more.

Yesterday I went downstairs to the gym and was on the bike and then worked with the weights. After finishing, I did my stretching routine. I had to take care of a lot of work in the building I manage, and the day flew by like the wind.

This morning I went to the park and jogged six rounds. That's two more than I did in the beginning, and I also increased my sprinting to six times up to the 5th tree. I really have to measure how many yards that is, so I get an idea how strong I am and how fast. I have to increase my speed. This is not going to go out of my head until I do something.

This afternoon after I left the office, I really felt tired. So I decided to take it easy and rest.

June 29, 2009

Did my stretching this morning and then went to the office. My coach called me today, and I am going to meet her tomorrow at the sand dunes in Manhattan Beach. I am excited! Now I am going to get some help with my speed. I went on the internet to find some information on starting blocks. That issue has been crowding my thoughts. I have yet to train getting off the blocks. Got some great information on how to increase my speed with certain exercises, and I am going to run this by my coach.

June 30, 2009

Woke up at 3:30 am, can't sleep. I am extremely nervous about my training. I feel like a race horse in the gate. I hope that I have been doing everything right to get better and faster. Today I will know after having a session with my coach. Gosh, this is the first time after the qualification last June that I am seeing my coach. I guess that's why I am feeling so wound up. OK, I have to get more sleep.

HAPPY 4TH OF JULY

July 4, 2009

On Tuesday I met with my coach in Manhattan Beach. I did my warm-up, and then she had me do a couple of sprints. She was extremely happy with my progress, and then we went to the sand dune. I made it up the hill once, and my recovery time was better than after one of the sprints. My coach told me that she is going to send me a detailed program for the coming week so I can concentrate on not only my running but also on getting faster.

Thursday afternoon I received the package with the elastic bands to do the isometric training, which will help me to run faster quicker. Right now I am extremely emotional, because in another 33 days I am going to be competing against women who have probably been running all their lives. I am pushing the feeling of fear away – far away from me. There is no room for questioning my ability to win. I can do it, I will do it, I am able. I can do it, I can, I CAN!

I started with the isometric exercises yesterday. For the first time I did two sessions of jogging today, and I realized that I was not fresh in the afternoon. Maybe next time I won't eat so soon before I go to the park. Could be that was the reason for feeling so sluggish. It seemed like I was carrying lead in my feet.

I am a little blue, because today on July 4th I am alone and have nobody to share the celebration. Oh well, that too shall pass, and tomorrow I am going to be busy with holding an open house in Santa Monica.

Something must have changed in my body, because I am constantly hungry. Now I really have to be aware of what I am eating, so I won't gain unnecessary weight but still nourish my body.

July 12, 2009

Another week has gone by, and I have been training intensely, more than I remember. Every evening I am doing the isometric exercises, and in the morning I am either in the park, downstairs in the gym or at home going through my stretching routine.

Friday I made it to the track at the UCLA campus. My coach gave me instructions on what to do, and I started with running around the track once, then did my drills to stretch. "Run 100 meters," she told me. Run 100 meters eight to ten times. Run the first 50 meters 60-70%, then just fly. So, I prepared myself, and I ran the first stretch, then gave it my all. I lost count. I believe I ran and sprinted eight or nine times. I didn't want to do more, because the last time I ran, I found myself getting slower.

So I picked up my sweatshirt at the beginning of the 100 meter stretch and walked over to the stairs. I couldn't resist; I jogged up two steps at a time, came down and jogged back up one more time. After that I slowly jogged once around the track. And to finish, I stretched.

It felt really good being on the track. What a difference from running on cement in the park. Wow! I really was going fast, and my legs didn't feel like lead; hmm, maybe the isometric exercises really help. OMG, I do hope so!

Yesterday I was on the bike for 30 minutes and then did some weights and the legs on the machine and stretching. My coach didn't send any instructions in the evening, so I freaked out. What was I supposed to do? I sent her an email asking if I will have to figure it out myself. Of course, she wrote back telling me that if I do that, then for sure I have to know exactly what I am doing. Anxiety, the fear of missing out on something, sat right on my shoulders and was wearing me down.

My coach wanted me to rest today, because next week she will have me on the track checking my speed twice, and I should be in perfect condition. I am not used to rest, so I am going to do what she is telling me. There was no way I was going to jeopardize anything. Four more weeks, and I am getting excited and nervous! Did I mention this before? Oh well, it is pouring out of me. What is going on inside of me? I am also very emotional lately. I miss my mother. She would be there for me, and I could put my head on her shoulder and cry and get that comfort I need right now. I can cry by myself, but it's not the same

Yesterday I went to a friend's wedding, and I believe I was the only single person there. It is no fun being alone all the time. Maybe I should have taken Moses, my cat, with me. Just kidding! It is so hot today, even he is hiding somewhere under a chair. Funny little creature!

July 20, 2009

Today I was on the track again with my coach. This time we were in Manhattan Beach at a high school track. The Redondo Beach track was taken over by a group of people, so we were not able to use the track at all. When I arrived early and realized that I wouldn't be able to run, my instinctual feeling was, why didn't my coach know that? Am I not going to be able to run at all today? What is happening? Why are there always hurdles? I was literally pissed off. I called and left her a message. When she called me back, she told me where to come and meet her.

Somehow I misunderstood the directions for the last part and made a wrong turn. When I finally saw my coach, she said, "You are killing me." That set me off, and I thought I annoyed her. So I started crying to release my frustration, which in turn set her off. She said, "There is no crying. If you are crying, we are not training. There is no crying in baseball."

That made me laugh, and we were able to discuss what happened. I explained to her that for me, crying is a form of release. If I can't cry when I feel that I have to, I hold every emotion in. Then it festers inside of me and makes me sick.

No more of this, no more! I was told not to cry during all of my childhood, and I am done with that. If people can't deal with me crying, so be it. I have considered other people's feelings for far too long. Now it is my time to be myself, and sometimes I feel like crying, that's all. It felt really good being able to explain my feelings to someone and find understanding. Holy Moses, am I stressed out or what? Frazzled, stressed and a nervous wreck. Wow, what could be any better than that while I start training on becoming a high-class athlete? At least I recognized it after my melt down.

I started by jogging around the track and then did my drills, then strides. And then I sprinted: first 60 meters, then a little more, and the fourth time I did about 80 meters. Of course I felt my "quadrothingis," and the fifth time was 100 meters and full out. Oh well! What can I say? Of course I gave it all, whatever was left in me, and I felt slower than the times before. Then it was over, and my coach asked, "Do you want to know your time?"

My answer was, "Sure, I beat Usaine Bolt!"

She said, "You did 16.1 seconds."

After I caught my breath I said, "What?" That was 1.35 seconds faster than my qualifying sprint last year. Wow! I was amazed and in disbelief at the same time. I really have a chance to win the gold medal, I really do!

July 21, 2009

While checking my email, I saw a message from my coach. She wants me to send it out.

Dear Ingrid and fellow supporters,

Ingrid Kern is a dedicated, motivated perfectionist. If she puts her mind to something, she will do it with all the strength and all the power in her heart and mind.

I have been working with Ingrid for some time now, and she has not only increased her strength, endurance and speed, she has reached a level that will put her in the running for grand successes.

All Ingrid needed was coaching and a little guidance - she carries all the right tools and natural abilities.

I am very proud to coach an athlete with such drive, intensity and dreams that I believe will be reached.

For the past few weeks Ingrid has worked on technique, bounding drills, calisthenics, speed and power. These have increased her strength, her agility and stride; stride length and force.

All of the above is done within a micro cycle; combining volume, intensity, cycling back to volume, and recovery.

Every workout Ingrid has given her all, going beyond any limitations. All her work is paying off.

K.C.

Wow, that is awesome. That letter is giving me enough confidence to believe in myself. Thank you. She is such an awesome person. I am so grateful for having her in my life.

July 22, 2009

It is ***hot*** today! Ten days ago I attended a wedding, and now I don't feel like partying at all. My emotions are rising every day; well, I guess e-motions have to be in motion…

Last Thursday one of my spiritual teachers, Panache Desai, came to Los Angeles, and I attended his workshop. It was amazing how my father was right there in front of me. As I held my hands on my forehead, he appeared right in my mind's eye. I stretched out one hand and gestured for him to leave. Enough of his appearances and his voice bothering me, hinting of not making it.

As it's getting closer to the competition, I am getting more nervous every day, and I truly feel that I have no reason for it. I keep looking for something to happen, and it is really very difficult right now for me, without anyone next to me and do everything in moderation to stay healthy. Being careful is not easy. Every day during training, when I feel one or another muscle, I freak out! I am so concerned about being in pain. The memory of it is very much alive.

This morning I went to the park and did all the exercises and drills and sprints my coach told me to do. My quadriceps keep bothering me again after the sprint. I am stretching and stretching, and I hope that all is well when I compete. If I allow myself to relax a little more and meditate, that lets me get in touch with my body. It feels really strange not to be moving all the time and doing just for doing's sake. I am a "Human being" for a change instead of a human doing.

While I listen to one of Panache's tapes, my mother appeared in front of me. My father was there, too. For the first time ever, I saw how she pushed him aside to make him leave. It was an amazing experience to see my mother protecting me. I am so grateful for that!

The heat is almost unbearable. My body is moving slowly, and my soul is yearning for companionship. I am dreaming of being caressed and kissed again. Christian has been in Chicago for so long, and I haven't seen him in a while.

Right now a slight breeze has found its way through the screen door and touched my back. I stretched my neck and decided to get a massage tomorrow. Oh no, not tomorrow, I am going to be busy; OK, Friday. I have to get someone who knows how to massage my tired muscles. Yeah, now this is getting exciting.

July 29, 2009

Ah, the pleasure of being pampered! It has been too long since I indulged myself in having a sauna, followed by having my body literally scraped and then massaged. It was heaven, and I enjoyed every minute of it.

I trained last week and stretched and stretched and...overstretched my hamstrings. What the heck am I doing to myself? I really was thinking that stretching more than usual would loosen my muscles. Grrr! Now I am angry, because I realize that the exact same thing happened to me last year before the qualification. How I was in pain with the IT band, went to physical therapy three times a week, but was still in pain on the day of the competition. Then I literally went out of my mind with fear that I wouldn't be able to run. But when the gun went off, I ran and had no pain. After the sprint was over, I didn't feel any pain whatsoever until – now! I better get my head out of my butt! Something is going on in my head that shouldn't be going on. This is becoming a joke.

Sunday was the last day that I trained, and I never thought I would say that I feel guilty for not working out one day. Today is the third day already, and I am thirsting to move my body. My coach and my physical therapist said to rest. Gee, I can rest when they put me into a box. Why now? I am listening though, because I do not want to hurt myself even more.

Eight more days, and I will have gone through the preliminary run. I know I am going to do fine, and I will be great on the track! Thinking about the sprint intensely, I start to perspire, and I am truly getting really, really, really nervous. I am going to win! I know it! I can do it! I will do it! Considering all the agony I am experiencing, the "overthinking" I am doing, all the positive affirmations I am saying out loud and writing down every single day, I wonder if there wasn't an easier way.

August 3, 2009

Late at night, after several hours of delay, my friend, mentor, teacher and spiritual guide, Master Inji Yong, landed in Los Angeles to keep me company during the next week. I feel like I'm being enveloped by a bubble, and I am actually outside the bubble watching me inside. I have to connect these two people to become one and do the best in a few days on the track.

August 5, 2009

Yesterday I received a lesson in *being* rather than *doing*. Master Inji Yong gently reminded me to take the time and meditate in the morning before breakfast. We spent part of the day stretching and exercising. After a light lunch at home, we took a walk in the nearby park. Later in the evening, we spent the time on my patio talking about life in general.

We got up with the birds around 5 am to get ready for the drive up to Palo Alto. It took me 5-1/2 hours with one stop and the use of my brand new GPS. Arriving at the Stanford campus, I parked the car, then registered for the events. Thinking about that, I was so sure I would qualify for the finals. Hmm, pretty cocky when I think about it now. It is, after all, my first national competition.

Anyway, Master Inji Yong and I went to the dorm where we were staying. After that we had some late lunch. The rest of the day went by in a flash, and I went to bed very early.

Insight - and then Out

August 6, 2009

Got up, had breakfast, spoke with my coach, got instructions on what to do, did my warm-up routine and then went to the track. Nervous again! Looked around; and was painfully aware that some incredibly awesome athletes were around me, which made me even more nervous. I only had one thought in my head: I had to qualify for tomorrow's final sprint. Again, I didn't know how to use the blocks, so I decided to start from the ground up without them. That was the way I'd trained for the past year anyway. I was scheduled to run in the second heat with eight other women. I had no idea how fast they were, and silently I was praying to make the cut.

Finally! We were called to the starting line, and I was in lane five. I realized that all the other women were starting with blocks, so I cramped up. Nevertheless, I got on the ground, focused on my lane, focused on the gun and off we went. I ran…this time no lead in my legs…I felt the shadow of the women next to me, and I ran like my life depended on it. I reached with my neck forward, and it was over. My time was exactly the same time as last year's at the qualification: 17.38.

What happened to the 16.1 my coach clocked for me in Manhattan Beach?

My friends at the finish line told me that someone else and I finished at the same time...you tied, you tied...I didn't believe it. I was absolutely certain that I beat that woman next to me. During the next half hour until the results were printed with the names of the qualifying women, it seemed to take forever.

Finally, someone came to put the sheet on the wall and...yes, I qualified. I came in second, and I will run tomorrow. I had another telephone conversation with my coach, who was absolutely sure that I would be able to medal tomorrow.

That evening we met with some friends for dinner, and I basically was mentally preparing myself for tomorrow. I already knew that I had no chance to win this competition. I had the 16.1 in my head, and I questioned how it could happen that I was still so slow after I ran at that speed I doubted myself, I doubted the time and I doubted my coach. Maybe she pressed the clock a second after I started? I was driving myself crazy. I had to talk to the voices in my head to stop telling me crap. Thank goodness I was a little occupied listening to my friends and telling them all about my training.

August 7, *2009*

I woke up early, a nervous wreck! I jogged for about 20 minutes, then went back to the dorm to have breakfast. I had time until 2 pm, but I couldn't wait to go back to the track, check in to get my lane number and then go across the street and do my warm-up routine in the park. I believe it must have been one hour before starting time that I went back to the track, thinking that they would start earlier than scheduled and I might miss the start. So I ran over there, put on my spikes and then realized that I had another hour. I changed into my regular running shoes to be able to walk back to talk to my friends, who came again to cheer me on. I just was so antsy that I went back to the starting line again, sat down in the shade, put my spikes back on and waited. I didn't know what to do with myself.

OK, here we go! It was the women's 65 – 69 age group turn to run the 100 meter finals. After speaking with my coach, I decided to stand, just a little crouching, that was how I trained. Of course, I was again the only one! Everyone else had their blocks in place. I felt so silly, but I got over it in a split second when the gun went off, and I ran. I only felt the woman on my right side, and for the life of it I was not allowing her to be faster than me, so I beat her. I came in 6th.

After some hugs and kisses from my friends, I walked back to the starting line to get my shoes and bag. I caught up with one of the competitors, gave her a hug and congratulated her. She asked me how long I had been running. I told her that I first ran last year in California, came in third and qualified for the Nationals. This was my first national competition and before that, last year's competition, I didn't run for 49 years. She said, "And you qualified the first time and you ran in the finals? That is awesome!"

Then, right there and then, was the moment it hit me. I took my head out of my butt, realizing that I had done an amazing job. I was really good, and I will continue to work out and will get better and faster with time.

National Senior Games - Palo Alto 2009

August 14, 2009

It has been a week since I had this incredible experience of competing. Following my coach's advice, I haven't done a thing, no stretching, no jogging, no bike, no stairs, no dunes, no nothing. She advised me to rest for three weeks. At first I didn't resist at all. Yesterday I spoke with my eye doctor, and I have to have surgery on 8/28. After the operation, I can't train for another three weeks, and that made me a little unhappy.

My coach is going to give me a schedule for the next two weeks, and then I will ***have*** to rest. Anyway, I am looking forward to next year's qualifications, and I am sure I will be less nervous. Now I know I have to focus on my speed and the start, and I will do better.

Yes indeed, it is the journey, not the destination, that keeps the dream alive. The thought to do better will get me to the destination. ***Oh, yes***!

October 2009

My beloved journal,
I have been missing you so much. Where have our daily meetings gone? I know you must be upset about my absence. I am so sorry that I got sidetracked by other issues that popped up. I know, I know that's what I have told you before. This time, though, it has been something that is really important to cement our relationship, and I promise that you will be happy. I can't wait to see you dance for joy between my fingertips when I sign autographs. You are in my thoughts all day long. I dream about you, and my heart sings when I think about your success. This is just a quick hello, and I will be back soon.
Your creator!

Sometime toward the end of 2009

Lives change, circumstances change and, of course, seasons change, too. I am alone, that has not changed. I don't have a coach anymore. She has moved away, and I am training by myself, which made me venture out into the internet and check what other coaches teach. I incorporated several new exercises – new to me – to make me faster and stronger.

I also began to think about more than just training and running. I pondered about health, wealth, sex and relationships. How they all intertwine and work together or not; and I immersed myself into learning more about myself – again.

Health

- Whatever you eat makes a difference in your physical well-being.
- Healing is as important, if not more important, than training.
- A balanced physical being is the result of eating a balanced diet.
- Abusing your body at times may show up years later.
- An injury may take years to heal.
- Your breath is your life.
- Every organ, every ligament, every artery, every cell in your body is connected with each other. If your thumb hurts and you didn't injure it, then you have to check what is connected to it and find out what really needs attention.
- Building a healthy body is like building a house; you need a great foundation.
- Good sleep is imperative. The body needs rest.
- A great warm-up will prevent injury.
- Everybody needs supplements.

- Body, mind, spirit. Health, wealth, happiness.
- Mind with body, not mind over body. It all has to work together.
- Mind-altering drugs are exactly what their names say. They alter your mind forever, and you may never be the same.
- Listen to your body. It will always tell you what you need to take care of.

Wealth

- Working hard doesn't mean you will get rich, it only means you are working hard.
- Being honest or giving your best doesn't mean you get rich.
- Helping people doesn't mean you get rich.
- Working long hours doesn't mean you get rich.
- Saving money for that particular time is imperative.
- Whatever you do in life, you always are selling yourself: your idea, your talent, your knowledge, your expertise, your beauty, your youth, your experience.

You have talent, knowledge, experience, ideas and expertise. Now you have to market it to the right group of people to sell it to them.

- You can't do it all by yourself; you need a team.
- Not everybody you like can be on that team.
- Everybody has to be focused on their highest and best value outcome.
- You have to search for good people, they don't happen to fall into your lap.
- The more you focus on one thing, the better you become.
- You need a mentor and a coach and a trainer and support and sponsors.

- You cannot trust that everybody is going to keep their promises.
- Timing is important.
- Trust yourself; study the actions of wealthy people and learn from them.

Sex

- If a man wants to have intercourse, it doesn't mean that he loves you.
- Sex has nothing to do with love.
- Tapping into your female sexual energy is more important than having sex.
- Being promiscuous shows little self-respect.
- Comparing sex to making love is like watching a movie or being in it.
- Having intercourse without loving the person is mindless and sometimes unsatisfying.
- It is more important to have a spiritual connection with someone other than the physical act of having intercourse.
- When you know who you are, the craving for sex becomes less, and the need to be loved turns into desire to love.
- All women are sexual objects.
- Men want sex, no matter what age they are.
- One more thing – sex is overrated.
- One more thing – get it while you can.
- Another thing – it's not that bad.
- Once a day – that's not real at my age! LOL.
- Once a month – maybe! LOL.

- Give each other privacy.
- Listening is extremely important.
- Hear what the other person says without having your own chatter and telling them.
- Allow your partner to be their own person and let them grow.
- Be supportive without being overwhelming.
- Be helpful without preaching.
- Be there without choking the other person.
- Be a teacher and a student at the same time.
- Be a friend and a lover.
- Be a companion.
- Be a parent and a child.
- Be open and honest.
- Give comfort where needed.
- Show compassion and encouragement
- Sometimes take a step back. You need your space, too, at times.
- Have fun together.
- Laugh a lot.
- Disagree if you believe it is necessary.
- Dislike the same things.
- Appreciate each other.
- Take a vacation from each other – ***alone.***
- Don't compare your partner with anyone else.
- Respect each other.

There are so many more points in the relationship department than in any other one. Well, yes! Of course! When you are dealing with another person, not just with yourself, there is so much more to consider. To make it work, it takes more understanding, respect, effort, care, discipline and lots of love.

If I'd only known all this when I was married; I probably would have done better. At the time, though, I did the best I could and the best I knew.

January 2010

Rather than writing and getting lost in thoughts about the past, I am going to take a break from pouring it all out on paper and start meditating. I realize that it is extremely difficult for me at times to let go of my past completely. I am asking myself if that can even happen. Situations arise when I feel catapulted back into my childhood, and then I freeze completely in fear and pull back. When I am in control of my thoughts, then I realize what I am doing, which then allows me to come back to the present.

When I am experiencing pain during my training, these are the thoughts swirling through my mind:

I can't run.
Something is holding me back.
I am angry that I can't train.
I won't be able to run fast enough.
I feel chained.
My feet feel like wood.
Something is gnawing inside of me.
I won't win.
Don't even try.
You are not going to run.
Enough already.
Give up.

Don’t try to be better.
Stupid thing.
I’ll give you some running.
Learn something intelligent.
Sit in the corner and watch how it’s done.
Go study.
You are useless.
You will never make it.
You are not worth anything.
What a joke.
You really believe that you can do that?
No, no, no!
Why not?
I won’t make it.
Others are better than I am.
Someone else will win.
I am not worth it.
I don’t deserve it.
No way, no way!
What am I – dreaming?
Why should I win?
I didn’t put enough effort into this.
I have to do better
I have to train more.
I have to feel the pain.
I am useless.
I have nothing to give.
I am not worth living.
Why am I even here?
Why was I born?
What’s the use, I won’t win.
Stupid idea.

I have my head in the clouds.
I am not realistic.
This is showing me that I won't make it.
This is the proof, what more do I need?
Get off it already.
Stupid, stupid, stupid.
I'll teach you a lesson.
First – study!
What the heck are you thinking?
When I say no, it's no.
You will do what I am telling you to do.
You won't run.
Get it out of your head.
I'll beat it out of you.
Stop crying, it won't change anything.
You'll stay home, that's all.
I'll break your back.
You will obey, or else.
You don't deserve anything.
The only thing you deserve is a beating.
I should have killed you when you were three.
You are useless.
You will never amount to anything.
I hate you.

In the silence of meditation
I recognized ME
Through forgiving myself
I was able to awaken my Spirit.
Unknown Author

Going Within

March 2010

Training for this year's CA games has intensified, and I will give it my all – for sure.

CA Games – Pasadena 2010

March 9, 2011

How was it possible that I didn't write at all for an entire year? I can only contribute it to the fact that I was absolutely sick and tired of writing about the agony I experienced and the stress and the fears. I didn't even want to be there with myself.

The only joy and incredible highlight of last year was when I sprinted into second place at the CA Senior Games and won a silver medal, clocking 16.8 seconds.

And then it was back to the state of depression. Ah, what a perfect front I put up, and how very dark it was deep down there in my soul. Fear of not being able to make it through the Valley of the Shadow of Death had me in its grip. Nightmares of falling into a dungeon and being swallowed by giant evil creatures made me more fearful of life. I knew something had to change; something had to happen for these dark and frightful times to change. I lived to go to work, train as much as I could, eat and go to sleep to wake up to another zombie-like existence.

After the National Senior Games two years ago, I didn't exercise for six months. I started again in March to prepare for the California Games in 2010. Without a coach, I went on the internet, and I was able to get information from several different running and basketball coaches and included some of their exercises, which lifted my spirit. At the CA games, I ran almost half a second faster than the year before. That was super exciting, and it told me that I can even be faster if I train for more than three months. I was pumped for a while!

So, this year I began again in January to prepare myself for June in Houston, Texas. As it went, I was enthusiastic. I stretched and jumped and lunged and did weights and stretched and jumped and did the stairs in Santa Monica and then...something happened. I stopped for a day, and then I started again, and then I stopped for two days, and then I trained for two days, and then for an entire week I did nothing.

Now I am at a point where I am disgusted with myself for not having trained all the way through the last two months and for the last two days before I started my routine. The voices in my head haunt me with, *So what's the difference if you come in 6th or even 5th? You still won't get a medal. Why bother then?* Screw it, I can come in third if I train hard enough and do all the exercises I have to and follow the plan. There was this pulling and pushing between this evil voice and the other one – my true me, maybe? I didn't even know. It was a constant battle, and I was watching it from the side lines. It seemed to me that I wasn't even involved; like I was observing a boxing match and was curious about who is winning.

Yesterday I started slowly and quieted the voice. Today I did an entire regimen, and I feel some soreness, but that's OK. Tomorrow I am going to conquer the Santa Monica stairs – for sure!

I know that this is going to be a little more challenging, because I am doing this practically all on my own, which makes it more difficult. Having someone telling me what to do and if I am doing it the correct way or if I have to adjust something in my sprinting, that would be extremely helpful. And the moral support definitely helped a lot. I have to cheer myself on alone,. That works when I am totally happy. There are days when I am not so happy and positive and all gong ho, so the cheering is more like begging to do it already and do it all and yes, the weights too…oh, I forgot the lunges with the weights – crap! You see, no cheering there!

I already started this year in a better frame of mind and do things differently, like I am taking care of my bookkeeping. So far, I am up to date with that. I am giving myself a pat on the shoulder, and this positive thinking will keep me going. All seems well in Ingrid's world right now!

For the next few months, until June 19th when I am getting on that plane to Houston, I will keep my journal again and share my feelings, my thoughts and what happens in my life going through this experience. I know that some people will be able to relate. If I can help someone to jump over their hurdles a little easier, get them to walk with a little more swing in their step and discover that life is full of surprises and inspire them to live their dream, then my journey and my sharing will have paid off. Until tomorrow!

March 10, 2011

I was going to get right into the things after I got up and was ready to drive to the Santa Monica stairs on 4th and Adelaide. On my way there, I remembered that I had a dream last night. I was driving on a very winding road in the mountains somewhere, and I was under the impression that I was driving within the speed limit. While I am thinking this, I see a police car pulling out from a hiding place and race after another car. I am looking at my speedometer and see I am at 35 mph. All of a sudden I see a speed limit sign of 35.

The light – now in reality – changes. I turn the corner and wonder what that has to do with anything I am doing right now. My thoughts wander from one thing to another. Am I holding myself back from getting better? Who are the police? Are they holding me back? Is it my father? You may say, those are silly thoughts. I say, there is meaning in every dream. I feel being fenced in.

I arrive at 4th Street, park, pull out my iPod, take my water bottle and walk toward the stairs. *Today is going to be easy*, I am telling myself, going down the stairs. I am listening to Earth, Wind and Fire and going up regularly, then down again. This time one partition is jogging and then walking and then jogging again. But in the middle of that part, I can't make it anymore, so for a split second I am surprised, upset, angry, disappointed at the same time. Immediately I switch to walking up and tell myself that it will be better next time. On top I take a swig of water, go down, and then do one step during one partition, then two steps the next time, and then switch off again. That goes well. Of course, on top of the stairs I am breathless, and I need a minute to calm down. I take off my earphones, because I realize that I can focus much better on my breath when I hear myself breathing – heavily, that is. Now I feel what my body is telling me to do, rather than focusing on the music.

Next I do another walking-jogging, which is better than the first one, and one step – two step. So, now I have finished five times, and my heart is racing, I am getting hot, so I take off my jacket, put it around my waist and think, *OK, I am going to do one more time. This time I'll do the jogging, walking, two steps and finish off with walking up.* Having had some water, going down is easier now than before. Honestly, I can't explain that…whatever! I do my 6th round of stairs, and when I arrive at the top my legs are a little wobbly. I get my water and walk to the car.

Now the voices are starting again. I am thinking about real estate, managing the building, my clients, and I am pissed off that this is going on and on and on. So I start crying in the middle of the street. Thank goodness nobody sees me – that's also going through my head. And I am talking to myself.

What's the matter? You did really good today. Stop beating yourself up! It will all come together. Focus on what you are doing at the time you are doing it, and leave the other issues for the time when they come up. But they are coming up now! Why am I thinking about them now? I growl and get into the car, still breathing a little fast but glad that I did my exercises.

Driving to the office to meet with a client, I am calming down. OOPS, I realize I have to go home first to change clothes. After the office I have to go to Sherman Oaks, where I will meet with a friend. He's asked me to share some advice about exercises to a friend who has some health issues. During the phone call I realized that I only can share what I know about nutrition. There is no way that I can suggest any exercises, because the gentleman has knee problems. I am very careful about suggestions. Not being a doctor, I certainly don't want to give advice where he could injure himself. I know too well what it means to hurt and then get physical therapy.

Busy right now, got to run to also prepare an offer on a property for one of my other clients.

March 11, 2011

After my workout this morning, I turned on the TV to find out if I can go to the exact space on the DVD when I fell asleep while watching it last night. I wasn't able to determine it, so I took out the DVD and switched to TV. This is what I heard:

"An 8.9 magnitude earthquake off the coast of northeast Japan spawned a ferocious tsunami that's caused massive destruction; flattening whole cities, starting raging fires, and killing hundreds."

I thought that I was at a movie channel when I turned toward the TV and realized that I looked at a newscaster. I am not sure how long I was standing there staring at the photos and DVDs from the devastated area. It seemed that time stood still, and I wasn't able to move. I pulled myself away after a while, realizing that I had to get ready for an appointment in the Valley.

Nothing seemed to matter anymore, everything felt so meaningless after I saw what happened in Japan. For a while, all my anxieties, my fears, my frustration, anger, impatience and dissipated in thin air. I kept asking myself, "What does it really matter?" How miniscule my fears, anxieties, anger, frustration and impatience became in the big scheme of things. All of a sudden it made me realize what a tiny spec of sand we all are and that a towering wave can sweep us all away in a split second. Wow!

This occurrence colored the rest of my day, and I went within. I meditated and prayed for the people in Japan. I want to be able to live my life every day like it is the last day of my life. I want to put a smile on someone's face every day of my life, no matter how I feel inside. I will do my best to live healthy and happy. And if it is meant to be, then I will do that for a long time.

March 12, 2011

Today I took some time off from training and did chores around the house. In the early afternoon I had some showings for the condo I listed for my client. Later in the afternoon, however, I experienced a rather big disappointment. A couple of years ago, one of my friends asked me to help her find a house, which I did. I provided her with the information about houses that were available in the area she was interested in. At the time we were not able to find what she really loved, so she informed me that she was going to stop and rent for a while.

We haven't seen each other in quite some time. When she called me and asked if I had time for tea, I invited her to come to my house. After a big hello and a hug she almost immediately told me that she bought a house last year, and she needed some advice. Her agent was terrible, and she didn't trust him. I looked at her with my mouth wide open and didn't know what to say, other than I didn't know about the purchase. I was disappointed that she hadn't told me. Then I remembered things she'd promised in the past and had never lived up to deliver. I always found an excuse why she didn't or wouldn't. Today, though, was different! It hit me! It hit me really hard, and I came to the conclusion that she was not my friend. Not because she bought a house using another agent. No, it was because she didn't tell me and then mimicked surprise when I told her she didn't tell me.

That changed something in me. I'd been in a similar situation before and had taken it personal. Now I realized that this had nothing to do with me. I was all right. I declined to give her any advice, letting her know that she should get in touch with her agent. I thought about how I have grown during the past year, how much stronger I have become and how more self-confident I am today.

It is really interesting that the phrase, "People are there for a reason, a season or a lifetime," rings true. I believe that's what the quote says…and when it's over, it's over!

March 18, 2011

Oh, my precious cat Moses left us Monday, March 14, 2011, in the afternoon. He fell asleep in my arms at the doctor's office. He was a very unusual and intelligent cat, and everybody who met him loved him. We had 15 years of joy, laughter, companionship and quiet moments. Now those times have ended within minutes. I am saddened, I am in disbelief.

I am mourning Moses, the incredible cat.

At the beginning of the year, I had an instant flash in my head that Moses was going to leave this year. Of course I shook my head and thought, *Why? He is totally healthy, and he is going to be 22 one day. No way!* Around Valentine's Day he became a little sick and stopped eating for a couple of days. *Must be a virus*, went through my head. He started eating again; only a little though and he became very quiet. Didn't eat the dry food, only his fish to which I added some pumpkin to give him fiber. He still greeted me at the door every single time when I came home. No matter how many times I left the apartment during the day, he came bouncing down those stairs and was either by the door waiting already or came walking around the corner of the living room to show me his love.

He always kept me company when I ate my meals. I gave him his treats when I had my breakfast and dinner. He stayed with me on the couch when I was watching TV and went to bed. Every night after I turned out the light, he got up from his blanket, came to me, snuggled within my arm for a while and then went upstairs to his bed.

Sunday afternoon when I came home from work was the first time he wasn't at the door. I ran upstairs, and he was lying under his chair. I lifted the throw, and he greeted me. I spoke with him and then left him there. Later he came downstairs and kept me company. At night when I went to bed, he was there, and he looked at me. I petted him and turned out the light. After a couple of minutes I felt him standing up, stretching, and I called him to come to me. He stood there for a while, listening to my voice, then turned around, jumped off the bed and left. My heart sank.

Moses hated the vet. When we went for a check-up last year, he was hissing and growling and needed a tranquilizer to be examined. I wanted to spare him that, so I waited another week, before it was too much for me to watch him hiding almost all day under his chair. I remembered my other cat, Mischa, who hid under the bushes in the grass before she died. I called the vet, and they told me I had to wait another week. I urged them to see Moses, because he was not himself. So, Monday I was there at 7:30 am.

On the way, Moses vomited in his carrier. He must have been so nervous! I carried him into the office, and the nurse told me to go into one of the rooms. After a while she asked me to get the carrier from the car. When I left Moses in the room on the table, I looked back through the glass window in the door. He looked at me as if he was saying, "Please, don't leave me alone!" It broke my heart. I have never ever seen a look on anyone's face like that. I came back with the carrier immediately, and at that point the doctor was ready to see Moses.

"He has almost no muscle mass left. He is still looking big, because of his belly. I will check his liver, his kidney and his intestine." I started crying, and he said, "Don't freak out! Call me between 1:00 and 1:30." With that I touched Moomoo; that's what I called him all the time. My Moomoo! I left, I got into the car and cried like crazy. I drove to see my friend, who comforted me, and I cried, and cried, and then I vomited.

I looked at the clock a hundred times, and finally it was 1 pm. I called the doctor. The nurse told me to wait, and then I heard his voice. "I am so sorry, but we are having massive issues..."

I didn't want to listen, so I asked, "Can I come in?"

"Yes, at 2 o'clock."

I got off the phone and screamed and punched the door and screamed and cried until I vomited again.

I asked my friend to please pick me up and drive me to the vet. At the doctor's office I went into a room and waited for them to bring in Moses. He was not a happy camper. He was hanging in the nurse's arm, hissing, and after she put him onto the table I was able to hug him. He snuggled with me as I was talking to him quietly. The doctor came into the room and he told me that Moses' liver completely shut down. He had three tumors on the liver. After the vet took a biopsy to find out more about it, he believes that at this point Moses wouldn't even respond to the medication.

His ears were all yellow, and I could see in his eyes that he was more there than here. I took him into my arms, sat down, put a little blanket on my lap and laid Moses there. I got his brush and, under my tears and calming words to Moomoo, I brushed him for one more time. He became very calm and snuggled under my arm. A few days ago he'd felt so healthy, and it seemed so surreal that he was ill and ready to leave. I asked my friend to take some photos and to give me some treats, which she held up to his face. At that point he hissed, and I realized he wanted his peace.

We called the doctor into the room. I put the brush away and held Moomoo. I told him I loved him and that it is OK. The doctor held his head, and Moses hissed a little while he was given the injection. Then he was quiet, and we rubbed his head. I closed his eyes, and then Moses was asleep. R.I.P.

These past few days were at times painful to live through. I felt Moses everywhere in the apartment. I thought I could hear him meowing; I imagined him running down the stairs, and the strangest feeling was going home, expecting him to be at the door.

I took some time off from work to get my head together. I looked through all the photos. I collected every single shot of Moomoo and scanned them. I realized that I could have taken so many more photos to combine them in a small book about Moses, the incredible cat. *100 Faces of Moses*, or *I Am Moses.* My little Moomoo, what pleasure you gave me for 15 years. Thank you!

March 28, 2011

Ten days went by, and I am not sure what happened that I didn't write into my journal. Well, maybe I do know. When I focus on the why, the answer pops into my head without a blink of an eye. It is right there. I am dealing with one of my other monsters! What am I saying? There is only one monster, and it is called fear. Yes, there is fear of this and fear of that, but it is fear that is the monster.

It raised its ugly voice and filled my head. *Nobody is interested in reading what I am going through, I am not important enough, I won't be* ***ever*** and on and on and on...

Yes, I worked out harder the last ten days. I incorporated weights and jogging, and I did my jumping. And when time came to write, the voices were whispering in my ear that this is really not important and nobody cares. Now I am saying, "Be quiet, because it is important that people who have lived with their monster know that there is a silver lining at the end of the tunnel. It is work, sometimes harder than other times, but it is possible to live a dream one has dreamed many years ago. Now is the time to share my feelings and thoughts, fears and desires and show that it is possible to get through all that crap from years ago and grow up and live without fear anymore!"

So, yes I was also mourning the passing of Moses. It was easier than I thought it would be. Still, at times I would sit at the computer and work and feel him right at my legs. One night in bed I felt him at my feet. I had to lift my head to make sure that it wasn't him. So, yes and yes and yes, if you ever have a pet and that pet dies, you will miss it terribly, especially after 15 years of companionship.

Besides training, I educated myself about nutrition and what is happening in the world about food and water. I learned a lot that I was unaware of, and to tell you the truth, getting too deep into the details is very scary. Now I am informed, and I can make choices. I don't like being ignorant and putting the wrong foods into my body, so I choose to listen and then check on what I've heard and google the information. Oh boy, it can get so confusing, and it is frustrating at times. I really would like to keep it simple, and I will.

Thinking about it and making that decision made me happier than I was a few minutes ago. Now on to the next chapter of adding some more information on how to get faster in running the 100 meters in a competition. I know a lot of people won't be participating in the Senior Olympics, and I am telling you whatever I am going through in order to reach my goal, live my dream/desire/passion some things/thoughts/f ears will hold true for your goal/dream/desire/passion.

We all need to look forward to accomplishing something in order to get us going. That desire has to burn in your heart, your mind, and your body. There will be moments, hours, maybe even days, where you don't want to do what it takes to get to reach that goal, and there is nobody else, other than you, who will do it for you. At the end of the month or year, you will either be stronger or still live with that monster telling you that you are not good enough, not worthy, not important, not who knows what. I think I don't have too much time left to listen to that monster's voice if I want to win a medal. I am going to shut it up and know that I will do what it takes to be the best that I can be.

March 29, 2011

This morning: stretching, jumping routine, lifting weights, lunges with weights, squats with weights, foam roll, stomach exercise, high knees, butt kicks, side to side walk, right over left/right behind left and reverse, A's, straight leg, sprint in place.

I felt really good after finishing, and then I went over last night's dreams. I dreamed that my younger sister died. My father and mother were still alive, and someone told me in the dream that because my sister died, my father will hate me even more.

This makes so much sense to me. My Dad died when he was 50 in 1952, my mother died in 1996, my sister died in 2003 at age 56. Of course he would hate me, because his favorite daughter died, and I am still alive.

So, what message was in that dream? Not sure. Then I dreamed I was in a building where there was a conference. Everybody was gone, and another person and I had to collect all these red apples and put them on silver trays. I mentioned that we could make some compote and the lady answered that the apples are not for us, which I knew in the dream. I am so confused and always looking for answers. Why is this happening? What am I supposed to do? Where am I going to from here? It dawned on me, children are always asking questions. Always. So, does that mean I am still a child? See, another question. Help! Now I am smiling and yes, I have to go to do some work.

A lot of maintenance in the building is keeping me busy today. Later I will do some work at the real estate office. I hope that one of the counter offers I sent to the agents will be accepted by the buyers and we can open escrow. That will be so exciting for my clients! On another note: with everything going on, I am still able to walk into a store and make people laugh. That makes me happy!

March 30, 2011

Got up at 6:30 am, brushed my teeth, put some cream on my lips, got dressed and was out the door into the park. I did my four rounds jogging around the park. Actually, the last round was running more than jogging, and I have to say, that I felt really good. A little out of breath, but good. No pain!

Then I summed up my thoughts during those four rounds. I was very aware of how my feet landed on the ground; I'd made sure that my feet were more flat than heel first. I was going over the DVD I'd watched last night about acceleration and what Mr. Mangiacotti was talking about. He is the assistant track coach at Brown University, and I got his program, which focuses strictly on the 100 meter sprint. So I was jogging and remembering what he was telling his athletes. That made me feel good! I followed his instructions, and hopefully I did things correctly. I am doing the best I can without a coach behind me, letting me know if I do something wrong. It has to do for now; maybe for as long as I will participate in competitions. For right now, this is all I have – myself. If I believe that I can do it, then I will do it.

After the jogging, I walked over to the cement walkway in the park and began my As, Bs and Cs, all the different walks and little jumps, and then I figured it was time to do a little sprinting. Three times about 30-40 meters, and I can't tell you how happy I am. No pain, no injury, no nothing! OK, now I am really happy and ecstatic that this year feels better than last year. So here I am, and from now on it is rigorous training.

Tomorrow I am going to the Santa Monica stairs again, and I'll see how far this is going to get me.

April 2, 2011

Oh yes! I went to Santa Monica on Thursday and did the stairs four times in 20 minutes. Still felt a little sore from the day before in the park, but it's all good. Did a short stop at the real estate office and then went back home. In the garage I bent down to pick up some paper and "crackle" – my left knee did something, and it hurt. Darn! Why do things always happen when I don't train? Anyway, I rubbed some Biofreeze on the knee and left it at that.

During the day I had to deal with some unpleasant business situations, which kept me busy, and I didn't have time to either, moan, groan or complain…LOL

My dreams the last few days are so confusing. I dreamed about my stepdaughter, who died in an accident in 2002. In my dream she was alive, and her birthmother was in the dream too, and she asked me for my address and phone number. So strange! Why are all the dead people popping up in my dreams now? Questions, questions, and more questions and no answers. Silly me, maybe I should stop asking and instead accept what is. No, I cannot accept some things. I feel the need to dig deeper and find answers.

I took off Friday and rested – from training, not anything else. Ha - look who came around to pay me a visit? ***Fear***! I checked my accounts, and the balances were absolutely perfect. Oh, what am doing to myself? I really am all right. I do have the money that I need to pay all my bills in time.

I am flying to Texas for the Senior Olympics, and I have enough money for the trip, the hotel and the car rental. I also have a little savings. Why is this happening? Even when all is well, I seem to be looking for problems/issues/challenges. Do I still have so little confidence that I can take care of myself, that I am making it?

When that monster is quiet and my sensible side is talking to me, I realize that after all these years I am still reacting like that child. My Dad's message was so powerful, making me believe that I was worth nothing; therefore I wouldn't get paid, even if I worked hard.

This is so sad, because in my head and heart I know this is not true. I'd already experienced success as a model and as an actress in Europe. Believe me these negative thoughts never ever entered my mind during that time. I never even imagined that I had a problem. My problem was dead, so no energy was wasted on dealing with anything that involved my father. The fact that I have to deal with those thoughts right now has to have a particular reason. I already know there is something left to learn, something I haven't touched on yet.

This morning I got up and did my in-home training. First I got side tracked by looking at my patio and seeing all the leaves and blossoms on the ground. I took care of cleaning up, and then I started stretching and jumping and push-ups and sit-ups. I did my As, Bs and Cs on the patio, back and forth. I even incorporated a couple of exercises that I learned from the new DVD and went to the roof to use my resistance band. That's to strengthen the hip flexors and make me faster.

Realizing that I am getting more serious about staying pain-free, I don't train until I hurt. I am also very aware to change what I do every day in order to give me a balanced workout throughout the week. I think I will make a schedule, so I have something I can look at and stick to. Oh boy, I wish, I wish, I wish…hmm. I wish so many things. Right now, I truly wish to remain injury free, have no pain anywhere in my body, and be faster in June than last year to win a medal. OK, lots of work to be done until then; still, I have to be gentle with myself. Tomorrow will be the park again!

April 3, 2011

My training in the park – I was very pleased that I was able to put in some sprints and felt really good after that.

April 4, 2011

I did my exercise routine at home including weights and resistance band – oh yeah!

Yesterday I dropped my car in Santa Monica to get new tires, and I jogged home. I didn't feel as strong as I wanted to feel, but I made it. Then I did my jumps and my other routine in the garage. In the evening I worked with the resistance bands to strengthen my hip flexors.

My head is filled with business thoughts, and I am in the middle of negotiating with my client and the other broker, who is representing the buyer. I very much know where my client is coming from, and I am doing my best to make sure he understands what we can ask for and what not. Again, it's a learning experience. Every deal is different. Every time I learn something new. No matter how long I am doing this, there will always be something I haven't experienced. This time I realize that I am much less attached to the outcome, and I know what has to happen, will happen.

Today I did a lot of stretching and weight exercises, and I was adding the jumping routine, resistance bands - it went a little easier and better than last night. Wow, that surprised me! We'll see how that continues. Hopefully, tomorrow I have my car back, and I can do the Santa Monica stairs.

Have been dreaming about Moses the past two nights, and I really miss my little Moomoo. As I'm sitting here in my office and waiting for my friend to drive me home, I realize that I am in a very funky mood. I am trying to remain calm and meditate and trust that everything will work out for the best and that I am protected. It is so difficult to get those other thoughts, which bring me down, out of my head.

I am going to meditate - I want to have a clear mind and be happy. I want to be happy. I need to be happy. I have to be happy. Yes, I have to be happy in order to get to where I want to be. And for right now, that's on the podium with a medal around my neck.

Indeed, that will be a happy moment. I am doing much better today than a few months ago. Working constantly on being aware of my state of mind made me eliminate some of the negativity in my life. More work to be done.

April 6, 2011

I am not sure where the time goes. Lately after I get up, I turn around, and it's time to go to bed.

April 7, 2011

Hmm...I still don't have a car, and jogging to the stairs in Santa Monica is way too far, especially when I want to do the stairs after that. So I decided I am going to sprint up the small hill between the street where I live and the Boulevard.

I am so aware of my arm movement now. It really helps to ***know*** that what your feet do depends on what your arms do. In the beginning, I didn't move my arms very much at all. I was used to having my arms straight at my sides from the time when I was modeling - well, that was another century all together.

After running up the hill, I jogged around the block to warm down. That was actually it for today, except I am using the resistance band a lot. Every time I walk by, I am doing 30 seconds and getting stronger hip flexors. I tied it to the bottom of my spiral staircase, so I don't have any excuse not to train with it.

I took care of a lot of paperwork at home before I was picked up and driven to the dealership. After that, I had a few frustrating discussions in business, and I am really focusing on staying calm and supportive to my client. I have difficulty understanding him over the phone. That makes me nervous, and I guess that can be felt. Meditation, meditation, and more meditation to become more professional and less emotional!

April 8, 2011

Not a lot to write about today. As I am sitting here in my office at 3:30 pm, I am going over today's events. I got up at 6 am and sent an urgent email to my client to make sure that he is signing all the forms necessary to open escrow. Then I got into my car - yeah, I have my car back - and drove to Santa Monica.

I managed to conquer the stairs six times today. I am slowly working my way up to do them at least 13 times, like I did last year. We shall see! My neck is bothering me, and that pain goes into my forehead. I am extremely stressed out about this business deal. Right now I am waiting for the forms to be signed and sent back to me, so we can open escrow. I am sitting on pins and needles, and I know the minute I have those papers in my computer, I will feel much, much - very much better; and for a while I will be able to breathe easier and go with the flow.

I miss Moses, my cat. I actually miss a family. Maybe I just miss someone with whom I can share what's going on in my head and not worry what they are thinking. Oh well, I am going through my five minutes of gloominess. That, too, shall pass soon. I do miss my Mutti!

That brings me to the relationship with Christian, which is no more and has not been for quite some time. How I was able to remove that from my thoughts so quickly and almost effortlessly surprised me. I am glad that I didn't look for any fault of mine that it ended when it did. I am grateful for the few times and the tenderness of it. Thank you for being special.

April 19, 2011

Where did the time go? I have been training and working and training and working and forgot that there is a life waiting for me to be lived. In the meantime, that time has gone by, and I can't recoup it. This is a vicious cycle, and I realize that as long as I am in this ridiculous backward-thinking situation, I will have to do something consciously to change my habits and my mindset. Otherwise, I will wake up one day and be dead and not have lived at all.

Sunday morning I was doing my stretching routine. While sitting on the floor and reaching forward, I heard a loud crackle. I felt a sharp pain in my buttock, and the rest is history. My physical therapist told me yesterday that I have a micro tear in my hamstring, and that means no training for a week. No stretching, no jumping, no stairs, no jogging, no sprinting – and my race will be in two months. OK, so I could just sit and write now, but that hurts, even sitting on a pillow. I feel like the princess on the pea! I am soooo very upset and I want to call my Mommy and cry, but my Mom is not with me anymore. So I have to cry by myself, and that's no fun! Not even my cat Moses is here to give me that certain look he always did and meant like, "*What now? Get a grip and snap out of it!*" I miss that little rascal! He was such great company.

When I am going over the past 11 days – I see my last entry was April 8 – I realize that those days were filled with a lot of anxiety and stress. No wonder my hamstring snapped. My therapist was right: I am tense and tight and stressed. Right now I am too tense, uptight, stressed out. I have no clue how to change that into being loose, bouncy, relaxed and not caring about anything but being happy. Besides being totally focused on my real estate deal right now and my training, I was able to tear myself away for a day and drive to San Diego on Saturday to attend a workshop with Michele Blood on how to access the light within, the power that is lying dormant. There is so much to learn and so much I want to do that it is time to prioritize what has to be done first.

- Closing escrow for my client's condo
- June – Senior Olympics, that means training and getting fit before it's too late.
- Creating a book: *100 Faces of Moses* or *I Am Moses*.
- Publishing my book *What's Your Monster's Name?*
- Finishing this book.
- Getting an illustrator for the short story book.
- Working on the fiction book I started years ago.
- Putting together the third poetry book.

I see that I am all over the map – again. Goodness gracious! And then I do have to take care of business. There are some things I will have to put on the back burner or cut out at all; to get my act together and be able to really focus on that one thing right now, which is the most important, and do it well and succeed. I am wondering if everybody is going through something similar. Do other people have so many things they want to do and then things get lost and not done?

OK, it's time to go to bed, so I can get up early in the morning and start my new life.

April 20, 2011

My birthday! Happy birthday to me! Thank you, Mutti, and yes, to you too, Papa, for giving me my life, for bringing me into this world, and for participating in making me who I am today.

From now on I will do the best I can to be successful and happy and bring more love, light and laughter to everyone I contact.

April 24, 2011

Easter Sunday - and I am in the office! I am not sure right now how I feel about that. When I think about it, this is what's going through my head: What is the difference? It's just another day. So what! I am choosing to be by myself. Well, not particularly on this day. I have chosen to be alone and take care of myself. Well, that's what I get - being alone. I have learned to accept responsibility for myself and my actions. This is a tremendous and important time in my life, and I truly believe that I was given the opportunity to be by myself to be able to grow and learn and grow some more.

Wow, life has changed a little bit. When Moses was around, I had someone to cuddle and talk to and feed and brush and take care of. That is gone now, and I do miss the company I had for 15 years. I was thinking over if I would want another cat right now. I realize it is a big responsibility, and I am not ready for that. If I would be in the market to get another cat, this time around I would need to get two kitties, because they get lonely when they are left alone, and I wouldn't want that.

Training: when I hurt my hamstring last Sunday and my physical therapist told me that I can't do anything for a while, the good old monster said, *"You see? You can't do it. You will never amount to anything. You always start something and don't finish it. You had to injure yourself, so you won't be able to compete."* And who knows how many more of these lies bombarded my brain and sank down past my heart into my belly, where they literally turned around and around in the pit of my stomach and hurt me for two days.

It made me sick, that I am still being bothered by those voices. During the last few days it became clear to me that they pissed me off, and I had to do something about it. Yesterday I did a 20-minute spinning class - well, it was in my gym downstairs in the building by myself. I had my earphones on and chose a few very fast songs, and for 20 minutes I pedaled like my life depended on it. Made me feel great!

This morning I slept a little longer, and after I got myself together I did my workout, except for stretching, and I really feel all right. Interestingly enough, my sit-ups were much easier to do than last time. A little rest helped that, for sure. So I am going to do the best I can and train and do what feels good, because June 21 is around the corner, and I do want to be prepared for the competition.

Reading through what I just wrote, something came to me. I recalled the interviews I did for my book, *What's Your Monster's Name?* Most men operate from their mind, but many women react to their emotions. It made me realize what happened within the last few minutes. When I leave my feelings aside, my frame of mind becomes very clear and actually empty, and I can make intelligent decisions. When I am feeling what is going on in my life, I become very emotional, and my reaction is somewhat gloomy. Hmm...quite an epiphany! It is so interesting that a little incident like this - writing right now - has such an impact. Although I was aware of the difference between thinking and feeling before, right now the realization entered my consciousness, and a light bulb went off.

Wow! My entire concept of looking at life just changed. We'll see how this will affect me tomorrow and the next day and if this "breaking open my skull" really has a dramatic influence on my dealings with life and people and situations. I'll let you know. Happy Easter!

April 25, 2011

I spent the majority of the day at the building showing apartments and having fun with people, making them laugh. Unfortunately, most of them are looking for something available in another month or two, and I would rather have someone move into the empty unit now than wait another month. I am lazy today, and I am enjoying the time I have to organize my thoughts and take it easy. Tomorrow is training day, and I am going to try a little sprint; I should be OK. It has been a week since I hurt myself, and enough is enough. I hope my hamstring agrees with my thoughts and won't give me any problems.

April 27, 2011

Yesterday was a good training day. After finishing all my in-house preparation work, I went to the park and jogged four rounds. Then I was brave enough to do three sprints. Only 60% — 80% to make sure I won't aggravate my hamstring.

It went well. I had to laugh, though. My left hamstring acted up like a spoiled little brat and let me know that I didn't pay enough attention to it for the past week. I rubbed both legs with the gel I got two years ago, and today I feel great.

June 21 and 22 are creeping up without me looking, and I am getting jittery. Even yesterday, when I was working out, the voices were there, whispering in my ear that I won't make it. I had to be really serious and told them to shut up already. I probably would have slapped anyone talking to me that way. Honestly, why would I slap myself?

This week is going to be a little more intense, because I want to make up for last week. I also have to be really careful not to re-injure myself. A massage will help, and I think I will do that on Friday after I do the stairs again in Santa Monica.

April 28, 2011

Nice workout today, and I am ready to do some more later in the day after my regular work day has been taken care of. Today is going to be very busy. Finally, my patio is going to be fixed, so the next rain will remain outside and doesn't find its way through some cracks into my apartment. I will come back to this later.

I had everything planned nicely for the day to be perfect and then – cancellation, or better, postponement of the repair. A few hours later, and they still were not here. I used the time to clean my entire apartment, took care of some phone calls to clients. Agents called, they wanted to see the unit I am in escrow with. Why now, why not when it was available? Sometimes I wonder about the psychology about this. Other than that – life is good. As much as I don't like that my carefully orchestrated plans were being shoved around, I adjusted surprisingly well. I still was a little disturbed by the fact that I didn't receive a phone call from the patio people. I am learning to be a little more flexible.

OK, back to work and know that it all will be for the best for everyone.

May 5, 2011

Oh my goodness, I can't believe how long it has been since I sat down to write. The past week has flown by as fast as a supersonic jet, and I am not sure if I am going to remember everything I experienced those days.

I did my training every day, I remember that much. I am getting to that point where I feel guilty if I do not work out, go to the park and run, do the stairs in Santa Monica -which I did six times this morning - do my weight training and some stretching – still careful not to hurt myself. My hamstring is not completely healed yet. Yesterday at the park, after I did my four rounds of jogging, I went again to the children's area, where the ground is covered with some material that is a little bouncy. I did all my stretching and jumping routine, and then I did some sprints.

It was darn hot, and my legs felt like lead. Goodness gracious, if that might be happening during the race in June, I can stay here and watch the competition on TV. Anyway, I hope that I am getting use to the heat. Also, I am going to run in my spikes, and they are a little lighter than my running shoes, so I will fly like an eagle.

I wish that business was this easy! Unfortunately, the escrow I was working on fell out, and I shrugged my shoulders and thought, *Well, onward and upward to the next.*

If that had happened a year or so ago, I probably would have fallen apart and had a nervous breakdown! How we all grow when we do work on ourselves constantly. I am really glad about my reaction to that incident, because it shows me that I do grow.

Sunday my brother-,in-law came with his friend to Los Angeles. My sister passed in 2003, and he met a very lovely lady he has been with for quite some time now. We only had about 2-1/2 days, so we were driving and running from one end of the city to the other end and beyond to get a taste of what LA is all about. They had a great time, and we had a lot of fun. It was really a very much-needed intermission for me from all the work and hustle and bustle.

May 8, 2011 - Mother's Day

How I long to be with Mutti
Hold her hand
Caress her hair
And whisper;
"Thank you for my life."

She left this earth in 1996 and still, her spirit and her love are surrounding me. No matter that we were not close when I lived with her, no matter we were apart in later years, no matter she was misunderstood by so many,

Mutti was the rock I could depend on – always! My compassion for her struggle, my deep understanding of her life's acceptance, surfaced only after I grew older and learned to live life.

Her own admission was that she came from a family where emotions were not apparent, let alone shown. She apologized for not being able to show love. She remained married, suffered public humiliation, and still was able to take care of me and my sister. This makes me aware of how truly deep the love for her children was. She may not have been able to hold us and tell us how much she loved us. She may have not known how to show tenderness, and all her actions seemed mechanical to me. Connecting to her seemed like a constant failing attempt. Mutti was there, a fixture in our home. Doing what her husband expected her to do, doing what she was supposed to do, taking care of the house, the finances, and the children, and be quiet and accept what was dealt to her. And if she didn't like it, she could go. Go where? Do what? With two little children after WW II!

Oh Mutti, how brave you were! I do realize that all the gifts and talents I have were given to me by you. I remember how you taught yourself English at the age of 65 to be able to communicate with my stepchildren; the few times you spoke Czech and French with Oma, your mother, when we were little children until Papa forbade you to speak anything but German when he was around.

I remember how you presented a delicious meal when only a little money was available and you had the most meager ingredients. Your tortes and cakes and cookies, your strudel and apricot dumplings, how can one forget?

How you bent and stretched and reached like a willow tree in the wind, and how I misunderstood that behavior as being weak. And! Most of all, your ability to laugh about yourself.

Thank you for passing these abilities on to me, thank you for making me strong and able to persevere, thank you for giving me the opportunity to laugh and love and, most important, share this love with so many. Your love for me may have been hidden from me. Your actions spoke louder, and today, I feel your love. Thank you, Mutti!

Happy Mother's Day!

I love you with all my heart.

Let's Get Physical

May 9, 2011

Into the park…oh yes, today was a good morning, and I am happy! I did my four rounds of jogging and then my warm-up to get ready for a little sprint. I still didn't measure the distance to make sure I run 100 meters. I know that today I ran maybe 60 meters twice and then, what I believe, was about maybe 100 meters or so also twice. It went really well, and I was able to feel how much easier and lighter my feet went off the ground. I am wondering what I did differently during the last week ,and the only thing that comes to my mind is that I rested much more – which, of course, I call being lazy – I didn't sleep any longer. I guess I have to accept that all the training I do is paying off – I hope! I will know for sure when someone takes a stop watch and clocks me when I run.

Today is going to be a good day – yes! Everything will fall into place, and all the remaining stress will peel off my body, mind and soul, and I will blossom into a successful, optimistic, positive, loving, happy human being. Amen!

May 15, 2011

I truly don't know how time goes so fast! By the time I can have a minute for myself, another week has passed. This last week was one big learning and growing experience, and I am glad that the right teacher appeared and helped me over that great big hurdle.

I realize that I am still facing my monsters, one or the other, every day. Sometimes they appear gently, or sometimes with some force. They seem to be right in my face. Sometimes they lean over my shoulder to remind me that I still have to do some work. They want to be acknowledged and put into their place, stroked or cuddled, whatever it takes to live with them in peace and not fight them. They are not going to disappear; I realize that now.

This is a very big difference from a long time ago. They only appear to frighten me if I let them, by falling back into reacting to something and not acting on it. Feeling helpless and alone will make a monster appear enormous, frightful and unmanageable. I still get stressed when I am sailing into unknown waters; now I am asking for advice, directions and support. And that big Mama monster is becoming less scary. In the end, it's curled up next to me like a tamed tiger.

My training has been getting better, my hamstring is not bothering me as much as a few weeks ago, and I am beginning to sprint a little further and do more repetitions. I started do more of the training in the park rather than at home. I am also aware that I do need my recovery period, and I am not beating myself up when I take a day off after a strenuous day of working out. Of course, that one little monster is telling me that I won't be able to qualify if I don't train every day. Maybe I could do more, maybe I am taking a chance by taking one day off too many times, maybe, maybe. Maybe the moon is going to fall on me! Without a coach and without a trainer, I am doing the best I can. Whatever happens on June 21 and 22 will tell if I did the right thing.

Having a goal and keeping my eyes on it keeps me going out there and training, keeps me sane and healthy. Knowing that what I am doing and sharing it with everyone is going to help so many people to get in touch with their dreams, and they will take a chance of being great achievers. I believe we all are supposed to live our magnificence and share it with the world.

May 23, 2011

A week of rigorous training passed. I conquered the Santa Monica stairs nine times within 55 minutes, and it felt great. The next day, I was doing home training – hahaha – stretching, jumping, weights. The next day I did a little jogging and sprinting in the park. I measured my stride to find out how far I have been sprinting, because I am not yet on the track. Hmm, 81 meters. I have to start doing 100 meters. Otherwise, I am not going to be experienced with the distance. I also managed to run up the hill near my house ten times and then cool down by jogging for ten minutes. Today was home routine, and later I may even go to the park.

I am more conscious about what I am doing and even more careful about staying healthy. I am getting to the point where I want to get it over with already, which shows me that my level of patience has not reached its peak yet. I still have to work on that.

Ha! I just scrolled through the pages. I was curious about what happened over the past two years. Wow…hmm. What can I say? Thoughts similar to how I felt two years ago are popping up in my head, but my reaction to them is a bit different. And the most gratifying result is that after training without a physical coach who would be telling me what to do and how to do it, I have taken the initiative to get virtual coaches and use their instructions on what to do to be a faster sprinter.

A few flaws may appear in how I approach my training or how often I do something, but I am doing the best of my ability to prepare myself for the competition in August. By reading fragments of this book, I also realize that I really love to write about romance, love and intrigues, and I am going to continue working on the novel I started years ago.

May 25, 2011

I went to the park yesterday. After I jogged around the park four times, I prepared for some sprints. I started slow; then got faster and faster. After six times I decided to stop. I measured the distance, and I believe I sprinted about 118 meters each time.

This morning I got up and I did not, did not, did not want to train. So I checked my emails first and then took care of my plants. A little voice in my head was talking to me. *Start your training. There is no reason why you shouldn't train today.*

So I started, and I did things a little differently today to keep from getting bored. I learned that doing sit-ups and letting out my breath really strongly made it much easier. I am really glad that I did my whole routine, including the weights. It took me a little longer today. I felt my lower back, and my legs were a little tired – maybe from yesterday – but I finished training. And tomorrow, I am going to go to the park again.

My head is full of who knows how many different thoughts, and I am at a point where I would love to go to bed and wake up a different person. I want to cry, I want to laugh,

I don't even know what I really want to do right now. I have so many projects on my hands, and it is so darn difficult to focus on more than what I am doing.

On the other hand, I would love to finish all the books I have started. Can't do that, because I am working on one right now. If I continue with the other one, I get confused, and then I mess up names and places – which I have done. I detected that yesterday when I browsed through one of the other novels I started a few years back. I didn't remember some of the things I concocted, and as I read further, I realized that some of the names were different from a few pages back…hahaha! So I changed and adjusted and corrected some of the mistakes, and now I have a project lurking in the dark of the computer, waiting to be continued. Honestly, I am excited about working on that book again.

Tonight I am going to go to church; I need spiritual food. Until tomorrow!

June 7, 2011

Santa Monica stairs – six times/32 minutes – not bad at all! I am pretty happy about it. Lately when I am sprinting, at about the second time I feel extremely nauseous, and I want to vomit. That feeling turns into anger, and then I want to cry. Of course because I am in the park, I am not crying! I sniffle a little bit, wipe my two tears from behind my sun glasses and sprint another few times.

This has happened twice already, and the last time I was thinking about why this might happen. Obviously there is something lodged within me that is ready to emerge, and I am holding on to it. I am not sure what it is and why I am embarrassed to let go and cry. Nobody is watching me when I run; and even then, who cares? I need to take care of that next time it comes up again to free myself.

I have been training vigorously the last week. Last night I was watching one of Marc Mangiacotti's DVDs again, making notes and then reading over them. This morning after my regular training I went downstairs into the garage to practice getting ready to start. OMG – I realized that I am doing everything wrong, and that cost me some time. I frantically made some phone calls to several sporting good stores for starting blocks. Of course, not one store carries them, so I had to order them online. I will get them on Thursday, which gives me nine days to practice getting off the blocks. At least I won't be feeling like some alien when I am at the starting line and finally using the blocks. I will put all my effort into doing it right. If I get off correctly, it may even shave my time, and I should fly like the wind!

I can't wait to get to Houston and see how much I have grown. Of course, that gnawing, relentless little voice sometimes rears its ugly presence and whispers in my ear, "Why do you think, you are better than before? Are you sure you did all you can do? You could have done more! You could have asked for help! Why didn't you do that?" And on and on and on. Sometimes I want to smash that voice and say, "Shut up! Why can't you be more positive and supportive? Why do you always have to put me down and make me less than I am?"

I feel, and I do know, that I trained more than last year. I incorporated different routines to make me faster and stronger. Of course, there is always that doubt about whether I really am doing everything correctly. I do not have a coach, and I do not have a trainer, someone who is standing next to me, telling me what I do right and what I do wrong. So I have to go with what I know and see the result of my effort June 21 at the semi-finals, where I hopefully will advance to the finals.

I am already planning on what to do next year to get even better. I will go to Santa Monica College and approach the track and field coach. Maybe they will allow me to use their track, and maybe they even have a team I can join. Something good will happen; I just know it. Slow down Ingrid, slow down.

June 10, 2011

The other day I did something in the park to get all aching and tight, so yesterday I did my training routine at home. At one point I finally let go, and the water kept flowing out of my eyes. I had to cry! I realized that I was holding all that stress inside of my body, that's why I am hurting all over. I am not sure why this is still happening. When I think clearly, I do understand that right now I have no reason to be stressed out. Why am I doing this to myself? At least it is not dragging on for weeks at the time...excuse me, that is not true!

I was stressed out over business for a couple of weeks or even longer. Then I relaxed about that for a couple of days and went right back into getting tight like a drum about my race. Good grief, am I ever going to learn a better way to live?

When I received the starting blocks, I freaked out, because I was completely confused about the placement of my feet. Why should I have my right foot in the front? After watching the DVD again and again, I finally understood that my right foot is going to push me out of the block. I decided that I was going to change the position of my feet at the start. That is a huge change, because for the last three years I've always had my left foot in the front. No wonder that I didn't get off correctly. In a way, it is a blessing in disguise that I don't have a coach right now, because I would have never ordered the DVDs and looked for more information online. I am so glad that I did!

This morning I was all ready, excited, anxious and nervous to try out my blocks at the UCLA track. My friend picked me up in the morning and off we went. Well, the track was closed because of graduation. The ceremony is taking place at the track over the weekend. I was bummed! No worries, I decided to start practicing in the garage. We drove back to my house. I placed the blocks against the back wall in the garage and began my practice. My brilliant friend suggested I make a video, so I can watch what I am doing after my practice.

The first couple of times felt uncomfortable. After that I got the hang of it, and I know that after one week of practice, I'll be fine.

I visited my physical therapist today, because my hamstrings on both legs are bothering me, my hip flexor on my right leg is telling me that I am doing something wrong, and my neck and shoulder are like a brick. Basically, he told me to relax. He said that I am too stressed, that I am going to be doing great, and that I have to heat my "hammies" before I do any training. They are extremely tight! OK, I will follow doctor's orders and relax to be better and faster.

OK, I feel better today after I worked with the starting blocks and saw the doctor. All I have to do right now is relax and meditate and sleep after that. Tomorrow is practice, then training in the park.

June 16, 2011

What a fast few days they were! As I mentioned in my last entry, the next day I went to the park and trained. And I ran in discomfort, but I did it anyway. I also practiced getting off the starting blocks, and I also did that in discomfort. I was feeling down and getting depressed and didn't know what to make of it. I've never felt like that in my entire life. Yes, I knew that I was stressed, but my energy level was always up. But now, all of a sudden, I had no energy, and that took me to a place of "dis-aster"! Thoughts like, *This is not going to be good. I am not fast enough. I didn't train right. I should have done this, I should have done that, and on and on and on.* What should I really have done? I didn't even know what! I started beating myself up, doubting myself, getting to be this three-year-old little girl who got spanked over and over again, because she didn't come to Daddy. I felt abandoned, alone, lonely and absolutely miser-able.

But I trained and practiced, because even with the voices in my head, there was no way that I was going to give up and give in to let them win. Even if I was training wrong, I was doing what I knew helped me last year to get stronger and faster. What if I put my foot down wrong? What if I landed on my heel? What if, what if...again, doubt was always in my mind.

I watched videos from Marc Mangiacotti, from Latif Thomas. And every time I saw something I could do better, I freaked out. With nobody at my side who was telling me to do it a certain way and correct me, I felt that my knowledge was useless. I believed that I didn't know anything. I was doing what I was told to do, and still, I didn't know if I was doing everything correctly.

Tuesday I went to my physical therapist again. He spent almost two hours with me, testing why, what and how things are with my body. To make a long story short, he discovered that I am fighting a virus. Mind you, other than my sort of a kind of depression, I don't feel sick at all. And I am extremely low on vitamin B12.

He did some laser on my left toe, which is still bothering me after what? Four or five years when I played soccer barefoot and stubbed my toe and never thought about having it fixed. Well, that taught me a lesson! I also got some laser treatment on my left hamstring, which was worse than my right one, B12 vitamin vials and some liquid "Immunoberries" to get the virus to leave my body.

After having such a challenge with accessing the tracks at UCLA and SAMOHI (Santa Monica High), I finally drove to the Redondo Beach Arts Center's track yesterday, which I have used during the past few years. It was a glorious day, and I was happy to be outdoors on the track doing my rounds, then my warm-ups and jumping routine and enjoying the sun and the warmth on my body. I practiced starting on the grass, because too many people were jogging and walking and running on the track. Oh boy! Once I almost fell on my nose; well, I really didn't. But I did something wrong to have that feeling of – oops, that was close – and then I continued for another couple of strides. I did not sprint, as I wanted to give my hamstring a little rest. Tomorrow morning I definitely will have to put on my spikes and sprint, so I can remember what it feels like.

This morning it was drizzling and sort of chilly, so I did the hill four times. Then I did one round of warm-down in the park. Maybe, if it is nice this afternoon, I'll do a couple of sprints in the park. I should do the starting blocks, also. Right now I am going to get one of the Chinese foot massages to get some energy flowing, and I'll see how I feel in the afternoon.

June 17, 2011

I am getting a little tired of having the pain in my hamstrings – yes, both of them. This is not making me happy. Last year and the years before, when I had any pain at all, my physical therapist fixed me in no time. Now this is taking longer than I want to handle.

This morning I did my home routine, then went to the doctor. He did some adjustments and laser to hopefully get me going. Started to put things together for the trip to Houston!

June 18, 2011

Today was absolutely crazy! I wanted to relax and finish packing, but no! Business called, and I had to go to the office. One of my clients wanted to make an offer on a property, so we took care of that. Then I had to attend to some issues in the building I manage – there went my screening of the *X-Men* movie. Oh well.

Honestly, when I make plans about just being and relaxing, so far that never works out. I am so curious about why that happens.

Tomorrow morning, my dear friend is going to take me to the airport and give me a great big hug, which is truly needed.

After the Games

June 26, 2011

Exactly one week ago, I took off for Houston, Texas, to participate in the National Senior Games. It was 67 degrees and cloudy in Los Angeles, and I needed to borrow my friend's sweater, because I anticipated 100 degree weather in Texas and didn't pack anything warm.

We had one stopover in Austin, and a few minutes later we continued to Houston. I stepped off the plane and felt a wall of heat hit my body. Oh boy! And I was still inside the airport.

After retrieving my luggage, I went outside to the rent-a-car shuttle. And there I was confronted with what was waiting for me at the track. It felt like I was in a pizza oven. I had no idea how hot it could be and how it would affect my performance. I got the car, then went to downtown Houston to register at the Convention Center. Next I headed north to Humble, where I had a room reserved in a hotel near Turner Stadium.

To conserve my energy, I didn't spend any time outside. After unpacking, I went to bed. I dreamed that it was drizzling, but after a short while the sun came out, and we ran in the heat. Mind you, in the meantime Houston experienced the longest and worst drought in decades.

Monday morning I got up at around 7 am, took a shower, got dressed in my running gear, had breakfast and drove to the track. Getting out of the car prepared me for the grueling heat that would be my companion for the next few days. I had to wait for quite a while until the track was available for training. I jogged around the track twice and gave up. It was dreadful. I was dripping wet and uncomfortable, so I went back to the hotel.

Tuesday I had an early morning breakfast and was off to the track. I was scheduled to run in the third heat. More women were running this year than two years ago. Waiting until the start was the worst period, and there is always some delay. I still don't have the experience to know when it's the perfect time to start warming up and stretching, etc., so I end up standing around and worrying and warming up too early. I hate that! There is a drizzle – OMG, my dream – and then the sun comes back out again.

Finally my age group is called, and the first eight women sprint. Then the second heat is at the blocks, and soon I am on the track with seven other women. I am getting the starting blocks ready when I hear, "On your marks!" I get down into the blocks, place my feet properly on the blocks, put my hands right behind the starting line and – "Get set!" I raise my body. Then I hear the gun, and I am off and running and running, and I am not thinking. I only know that I am in front and OK, then I am still in front, and I win the heat. I am dripping sweat. I am red like a tomato, and I could have cooked an egg on my forehead.

When I hear the time, I am in utter shock. I ran slower than my worst time in my previous competitions, 17.91. How did this happen? What did I do wrong? I am completely upset. But at least I won the heat, and I qualified for the finals – wait. Oh no, they are telling us 16 women qualified for the semi-finals; we only ran prelims. Why, what, how? Well, we protested. The official told us to be there the next day at 8:30 am, and we'll see what happens.

I get up Wednesday morning, open the curtains, and see clouds in the sky and wet streets. Oh good, it won't be that hot! After breakfast I get into the car and drive over to the track. Meanwhile, rain pours from the sky, accompanied by thunder and lightning. And it is freezing cold. All events are being postponed for half an hour every time there is lightning within eight miles. I am jumping around to keep warm. It's 67 degrees – just great!

Around 11:30 am, we are finally getting on the track. Rain is still coming down in buckets, and everybody is soaking wet. OK, I am in heat two. Four of the women sprinting with me are way faster than I am. So again, I am bummed but determined to give it my all and my best!

I prepare to get settled into the blocks. Rain drops run down my face. A strand of hair slips over my eyes, and in a daze I move it back. I lick the water off my lips. My hands are positioned. I am on the ground – I am ready.

I hear the gun. I lift my body, pushing off the blocks. I feel that I am pushing and pushing and all of a sudden – it must have been the fifth step - I feel an unholy sharp pain at the end of my butt. I hear a crackle, and this is what went through my head: *OMG, I am in so much pain, I can't make another step, I can't run.* And at the same time, I hear my father's voice at my right ear: *Run, just run!* I thought I was standing still, and it felt like I was in slow motion. But in reality, it truly only was a split second.

So I run and run and see the woman on my left in front of me and I push and I am in pain and I run past her and then the race is over. I am so ready to cry – no, scream. I am so much in pain.

Rain is still coming down, soaking my running gear and making my hair dripping wet. I hobble back to the starting line, and I hear the announcer telling us to clear the track and the infield. More lightning is nearby, and we have to wait for the finals. I get my sweater, which is wet, too. Then I take off my spikes and barely make it to the area where the results are placed to see the damage I have done.

We are told that the two heats were not the prelims, they were the finals. The top times from both heats were combined. So, with my lousy time of 18.59 seconds, I was seventh overall. I am not happy about that; on the other hand, at least I finished and still made it within the top eight. In the end, that would have given me a chance to compete in the finals.

After returning to the hotel, I immediately called my acupuncturist, who told me that I had to see him the minute after I land in L.A. I was in excruciating pain and was ready for some rest.

In conclusion, I decided that I will have to get a trainer, because without any supervision I have no chance on earth to get a medal at the National Games. And that is truly my reason in participating. I want to win! I know it is great that I am able to participate and get this far, but a medal is a medal, and nothing else counts as much.

I also realized that whatever happened to me when I was 16, when I was not allowed to run and do sports, that chapter was closed. Look, here was my Dad telling me to run. That was awesome, and with tears in my eyes I say, "Thank you, Papa!" Now I can leave that pressure behind me. I don't have to prove anything to anybody anymore other than to myself, and that is a different monster altogether.

Whatever you do, whatever your desire, whatever your dream, follow it for the right reason and with a passion that won't allow you to quit.

July 9, 2011

What an emotional journey I took since the last time I shared my thoughts and my feelings with these pages. Upon my return home, I went to the acupuncturist to get help with my injured hamstrings. I told him what happened, and he recommended a sprint coach for me. I called him and met with him the next day at Urth Café in Santa Monica.

He seemed very knowledgeable, and he recommended that we take care of the hamstring, doing basic core exercises, so I won't end up with too much scar tissue. I was all excited!

That was on a Monday. Tuesday we met at my building's gym, and the trainer also looked at the video from the competition. He showed me how I used the outside of my feet, not the entire foot. He explained to me how the muscles shifted and that caused the injury. Of course an expert can explain that much better, but that's all I remembered, because what he said afterwards made me all excited and ready to run at that moment. He told me that he would retrain me how to run, and he could get me to run the 100 meters in 15 seconds. My head went ding, ding, ding! Fifteen seconds? That's a gold medal! Oh my goodness! Whatever it takes! I'll do whatever it takes. I was so excited that I forgot all about my injury. I felt like Superwoman. I can do that. I will heal in a flash – or so I thought.

Thursday I was on the track, and I was still hurting. Friday was acupuncture, Saturday was on the track with core exercises; no running, no jogging, just stretching and bending.

The pain did not go away. I wasn't able to sit longer than five minutes. Even walking faster than normal caused me pain. I didn't want to believe that I couldn't heal faster than other people. What happened? All the other times physical therapy and acupuncture helped and now…I was told that a tear in my hamstring might take a year or even longer to heal.

Tuesday morning I was on the track again, and suddenly it hit me: I was angry! Something was cooking inside of me, and I didn't know what it was. I wanted to scream, cry, hit something, someone. I felt like howling! I conveyed my feelings to my trainer, who suggested that I discuss it with him. But I wasn't able to do that, because I didn't even know why I was angry and what it was about. We ended the training session. I drove home, and after a shower, I went about my day. Mentally and emotionally exhausted, I went to bed early.

When I opened my eyes Wednesday morning, I sat up and, like a ton of bricks, it hit me. The connection between my physical pain and the abuse of my childhood was right in front of me, and I started crying. I didn't want to go there again. I thought I was done with that. I truly believed that I had put that pain behind me, put it in a box, wrapped it tight and placed it high on a shelf where it couldn't reach me anymore. But now it was staring me in my face, actually making me feel the pain in my hamstrings. I said, "No way, not again, not anymore! I do have a choice now. I am not helpless, I am not being beaten, not kicked, not thrown down a flight of stairs. This is my life, and I am going to stop that pain right now."

I called my trainer and told him my decision. I was not sure about his thoughts, and I honestly didn't care. This was not about pleasing him. This was about me not being in pain. Of course he told me that my pain was really only discomfort and after a while I wouldn't feel it at all. I was not about to argue that with him, because who knows, maybe my pain level six is his level three.

I cried, and I was sad. But the next day when I was less emotional, I did some research on hamstring injuries. I learned that even when I don't feel any pain anymore, a hamstring injury never heals completely.

I was thinking about the last five years; when I first started training and how my right hamstring bothered me before the first competition. Then the following year how it became a little more painful and the third year how I must have pulled it when I was training on the Santa Monica stairs. For a moment or two I thought I would never even walk, I was so much in pain. But then my physical therapist performed a miracle, and I was without any pain.

Last year my left hamstring started to act up too, sometimes. I had a little more intense pain, but that went away quickly, because after each competition I didn't exercise for six months. I always prepared myself for only three months. Well, this time around I was training intensely for six months. I pulled my right hamstring first and then my left one, too. Now I understand that sprinting with my feet not firmly on the ground but a little twisted did all that.

Then I thought about the possibility of running the 100 meters in 15 seconds and what would be involved: It would require at least an entire year of relearning how to sprint properly; an entire year of physical, emotional and financial sacrifice, sweat and tears and possible injuries; an entire year of worries not to make one wrong step. And then what?

It made me realize that I had a choice, a choice of being nice to myself, loving Ingrid. I could love her as who she is, what she did, with all her faults, what she accomplished, her talents, her love for people, her compassion, the joy she shares with the world. Ingrid, the little girl inside of me, who wants to be loved.

Or I could continue to get hurt, physically and emotionally. Only this time, I was going to do it to myself. Now, this is the true reason why I decided not to sprint anymore. The sacrifice didn't justify the payoff, especially imagining the possibility of a more serious injury. It didn't make any sense. As much as I was prepared to continue and how thrilled I was with the idea of winning a medal at the National Games, I am committed to be nice to myself and stop beating myself up. I have been bad to myself in small ways and bigger ways for so many years without realizing it, because I was used to the physical abuse and it felt so familiar. Now it became too much and my body said, "No more," and this time I am listening. This time it is my voice who is telling me what to do, and I am listening. This time I trust myself, and I am not thinking, *Well, my trainer knows better than I do. He is smarter! Who am I?*

In a way, I am sad that this chapter is closed. On the other hand I fulfilled my teenage dream to participate in the Olympics. So what if it was the Senior Olympics? I competed, and I did well, and it is amazing to me what had to happen to make that jump from being obsessed with something to being OK giving it up. I know it will take some time. And of course, when my hamstrings have healed, there will be that thought, *Maybe I could try one more time.* Then I will have to be smart and remember what I am going through right now. I need to remember the pain in my leg when I am sitting, the pain in my hamstring when I turn over in bed; that sharp knife-like pain in my upper thigh when I slip. And hopefully, I will have the intelligence and willpower to say ***no***!

No to pain. No to abuse, whether it's physical, mental, emotional and psychological. No more!

Enough!

It is now February 2013, and I have managed to stay off training and exercising since August 2011. Watching Usain Bolt last year at the Olympics was exhilarating and the urge to compete again was very quickly whisked away, understanding that it would harm me physically. My left hamstring is still bothering me when I jog across the street, so running is not an option at this moment.

I am looking into getting into Tai Chi again, because my body is yearning for movement.

Looking back on my journey makes me realize today how important it was for me to have the chance to participate in the Senior Olympics, tame that monster called ***fear***; and now go on to make my next dream come true.

Not so fast! The pain in my left leg didn't let me put the chapter to rest. I didn't realize that I had more work to do, more work on taking care of my physical being. I truly believed I was done when I connected the pain to the abuse. No, it was just another beginning of peeling back the veil and going to work.

Acupuncture, physical therapy, internists, Pilates, more doctors to find out what is happening with my leg. Finally another doctor prescribed an MRI, which my physical therapist had wanted in the first place and this is the result.

Two of my lower discs are deteriorating and bulging. I have a fractured disc. One of my nerves is pinched, which causes the pain in my left leg. All the different therapies I tried made the pain even worse.

April 2013

I met a healer who is doing Bowen Therapy, which has to do with shifting energy in your body. Of course, something came up – again! He told me that the back is my past, and my past is holding me back. I am stuck in my past. I really didn't want to hear that, because I believed that I had worked enough on my issues with my Dad and there was nothing left to discover, chew over, forgive; and what not. I was done with that. I truly was.

Well, the day after we had a two-hour session, I got up in the morning and did some stretches. While I was in the shower, all of a sudden it went POP in my head. My mother was there, and for the first time ever I thought, *Why wasn't she protecting me that day when I was three and my father beat me so hard that I urinated on his lap and then he beat me some more. Only then did she say, "It's enough!"* I was standing in the shower, staring at the wall, crying, questioning why, why, why. Then I coughed and cried and screamed, and I vomited.

I am in agony. I am in bed. My shins are burning like hell, my hip flexor muscle is pounding, and I am ready to throw up again. No matter how I shift my legs, the pain is there, and it is consuming me. It is inside of me, eating away what's left of my positive outlook on life. I am reaching a point of not being able to be – to be me.

Life has been extremely difficult while I am feeling fire ravaging my leg. Demons seem to be dancing inside of me, slicing my knee with their swords and making an effort to determine who is winning the battle of how much they can hurt me even more. This is it. I cannot and will not write anymore about this. I am done.

October 2013

After nine months of agony, with pain accelerating to sheer horror, after hoping and praying that people will be able to help me, I have finally come to the realization that only one person will help me. And that is ***me***! I had to trust my instincts. I had to make the decision to get surgery. I had to stop searching for an answer from someone else, stop believing that they know better. I had to go so far down, to feel so much physical pain to reach the point where I couldn't take it anymore. I asked myself why I needed to do that before I stopped. Being confined to sitting in a chair, taking only a few steps without feeling pain and lying in bed half the time was not my idea of living. As my mother would have said, "It's enough!"

I'd believed the voice in my head that said the doctors know better than I do because they are smarter than I am. They have a degree, they studied, and I am stupid. That thinking got me to this point, and I realize how I listened to the voice in my head rather than trusting myself, my instincts and could not hear my body talking to me. I was so deep in the hole, I still listened to my Father's voice. I looked at people for an answer and tried every doctor they recommended and wondered why nothing helped and only made my situation more unbearable.

I even trusted my internist, who told me I should take Celebrex and I wouldn't have any side effects, when I do not like any kind of medication Well, I did! One morning I got up. After my shower I looked into the mirror and didn't know who

I was, didn't remember my name, in what country I lived, what language I was speaking. I freaked out. After a couple of minutes things came back to me slowly, so I was able to make a phone call. The doctor told me the next day it was not the medication, that I was stressed. That was the last time I saw that doctor. My body was talking to me loud and clear, and it forced me to listen.

When I was crawling on the floor in my living room one day, curled up like a baby as I tried to find a comfortable position while the pain ravaged my leg, something snapped in my head, and it brought me back to the present. I realized that this is my life. I am an adult. I can make my own decisions, and I do not have to depend on anyone to make my decisions. I can do that all by myself. And if I make the wrong decision, then it was mine and not anyone else's. I am smart, I am strong, I am awesome. And I am going to take control of my life. Right here, right now! It felt as if I disconnected from the umbilical cord that tied me to my father.

October 22, 2013

It was the turning point in my life when I had the micro discectomy to repair the damage that was done to me so long ago and to get me back to live a life without pain.

I'd made this monster sever from the past to become who I am supposed to be. No more fear! No more pain! Not from anybody, and especially not from me.

Epilogue

August 2014

Almost a year has passed since my surgery, and I feel great. No more pain in my leg, no back pain, and I've enjoyed reaching a level of growth and understanding that yes, it is the journey that is important. These past months have given me a chance to also learn when to avoid confrontations, which would take me back to my childhood and I'd react like that little girl. The time since I started training in 2007 was needed for me to understand that every time I felt physical pain or had negative thoughts and voices in my head was a remnant of my childhood.

After my father beat me or punched me, I never knew when to expect the next blow. When I came home with a great report card, his response was that it was expected. Five minutes later he would find a reason to abuse me. *Show me how your piano lesson went this week.* Already afraid of him, I sat down and played Beethoven's *Fuer Elise*. In the middle of it I touched the wrong key and ***bam***. He smacked my head, I slipped off the piano stool and his shaking voice whispered, *You fool, will you ever learn?* He picked me up from the floor and slammed my body back on the stool.

Of course, a psychologist would have gotten me to understand that sooner. Maybe. I am glad that I got it, and I am glad that I went through the experience. It showed me how much dedication, commitment and perseverance it takes to become great in doing anything.

Yet some triggers still make me catch my breath at times. I turn away. I do not feel the need to defend myself anymore. Now I have tamed my monster. What a run it was! It is done – finally!

Some rather difficult confrontations with people made me decide to make an appointment with a psychologist. I am now getting guidance and assistance in dealing with life like a grown up. My first session was amazing and I am so glad to have found someone I can trust. It is nice having support. Once in a while I will access that support. Thank you!

About the Author

After being denied the opportunity to participate in the preliminary try outs for the 100 meter sprint, shot-put and long jump at the 1960 Olympics, it took Ingrid almost 49 years to reconnect with her dream. She started her training in 2007 and sprinted into third place at the 2008 California Senior Games to qualify for the National Senior Games in 2009.

Confronting her monster, which laid dormant for so many years and hidden from her consciousness, she dug deep into her psyche to heal the pain afflicted so long ago. Endless strings of horror surfaced, and it took enormous courage, determination and strength to go through the process of healing.

Coming out whole and renewed, Ingrid found out who she really was, what she was capable of accomplishing and how to quiet the voices in her head that made her believe she was worthless. This gave her the self-confidence she'd never had.

Triumph is the follow up book to *What's Your Monster's Name?*, in which she interviewed people who told her how they applied a certain life skill to overcome difficult situations.

Her abusive and alcoholic father, who died at the age of 50, left a completely unsuspecting Ingrid. She did not know that she would carry the burden of "monsters" for many years. The monster of fear! Fear of being stupid, fear of not being good enough, fear of never accomplishing anything, fear of everyone knowing better and more than she did, which finally got her to the realization she does accomplish things and when it comes to her body, mind and spirit, she knows best.

Over the years Ingrid realized that she was not the only one who has been abused. By sharing her experience, her emotional journey to self-discovery and healing the wounds, she shows that one can shed the burdens of the past.

Ingrid lives in Los Angeles and spends her time working in real estate, managing a building, writing and traveling.

CPSIA information can be obtained
at www.ICGtesting.com
Printed in the USA
FSHW04n1611300318
46111FS

9 781457 549915